HOW TO ANALYZE
PEOPLE 101

By

ROSS DAVIES

are periodically made to this book as and when needed. Where appropriate and/or necessary, you must consult a professional (including but not limited to your doctor, attorney, financial advisor or such other professional advisor) before using any of the suggested remedies, techniques, or information in this book.

Upon using the contents and information contained in this book, you agree to hold harmless the Author from and against any damages, costs, and expenses, including any legal fees potentially resulting from the application of any of the information provided by this book. This disclaimer applies to any loss, damages or injury caused by the use and application, whether directly or indirectly, of any advice or information presented, whether for breach of contract, tort, negligence, personal injury, criminal intent, or under any other cause of action.

You agree to accept all risks of using the information presented inside this book.

You agree that by continuing to read this book, where appropriate and/or necessary, you shall consult a professional (including but not limited to your doctor, attorney, or financial advisor or such other advisor as needed) before using any of the suggested remedies, techniques, or information in this book.

TABLE OF CONTENTS

INTRODUCTION

Throughout the years, analyzing people as I approach them has been so easy for me. I see it as a skill, although it's just something that I accidentally learned throughout my teenage years when I started working at a restaurant as a server – I would look at people who enter the facility and guess what would they order, how much they would spend, and how they would treat the staff – I was almost always correct, and throughout the years, it just developed. Yes, I know how funny it sounds when I tell you how it all started and how I even consider it as a skillset. However, it wouldn't take long until you see how beneficial it could be for anyone.

After all, today, in order to be truly successful in leadership, politics, or any kind of negotiation, sales, business, and diplomacy, being able to learn how to analyze people would be truly beneficial. If you would like to find means to improve your career, it's important to learn how to read people's character and body language.

1

This book will teach you how to do this. By the end of this book, I hope you'll realize how easy it is to analyze a person by simply knowing where to look. By understanding what's really going on inside of them, you will see that influencing, persuading, and controlling them is fairly achievable.

You can do that by being able to know how to recognize a person's specific personality patterns and ways wherein they construct their internal experience.

For example, you are able to identify whether the person in front of you can take pressure well and can make himself calm during a stressful situation.

A great part of our lives will be spent getting on with others. We go on with our lives more efficiently if we can relate and connect well with people. And of course, life would be easier if we can easily know what goes inside the mind of the person in front of us and what kind of person they are in general.

In this book, you will learn an extremely practical system for rapidly determining the kind of person you are trying to deal with and how you are able to make the most out of your interaction. You'll discover how to connect with people in ways that they're going to respond to positively and just as significantly, how to evade useless misunderstandings.

This book, however, doesn't only focus on teaching you how to analyze other people, but also how you can analyze yourself to become aware of things you probably don't know about yourself as well as to celebrate your distinctive strengths.

This is also going to provide you with a pattern that will help you comprehend the different types of people you will get to encounter on a daily basis and how you can deal with them.

CHAPTER 1

ANALYZING YOURSELF

"Love yourself first before you love someone." This is a cliché we always hear when it comes to loving someone. This is true.

But to love someone, you need to know them. Not knowing yourself means not knowing your limits. This will heavily influence the level of your accomplishments as well as possibly aggravate your future plans.

A lot of people have wasted resources and efforts just because they didn't know what their limitations are. This is why analyzing yourself as well as your circumstances before doing something is vital.

The "self-analysis" must be all-embracing; it has to be done in every situation you will be in.

1.1 How to analyze yourself and understand what's going on in your own mind?

It's our human nature to constantly grow and change based on our personality and experiences. This is why it's imperative to take the time to perform self-analysis. This exercise will help you reflect on where you are in different aspects of your life. Together with this information, you can easily make essential adjustments and changes as you carry on and move forward in your life.

PART 1: EVALUATING YOUR SELF-ESTEEM

Step 1: Consider your childhood experiences. It's not always easy to understand who you are as a person and why you do things a certain way. Much more, what drives behavior and self-perception is our subconscious beliefs and attitudes. It is important to look deeper if you want to know how you really see yourself on a subliminal level. Here are important questions you must answer to know yourself better:

- ❖ Growing up, do you think you were listened to enough, or were you severely criticized?
- ❖ Were you spoken to with respect, or were you ignored or made fun of?
- ❖ Did you get enough affection and attention, or were you neglected?
- ❖ Were you abused physically, sexually, or verbally?
- ❖ Were you recognized for your accomplishments?
- ❖ Were your failures and shortcomings accepted or criticized?
- ❖ Were you pressured to be perfect?

By answering these questions, you will know where your attitudes or beliefs might be coming from. Walk down your memory lanes and relive your life as a child.

Step 2: Monitor your moods. For a whole day, carry a journal with you. Every time you feel a change in your mood, immediately write it down. This would be a way for you to identify your internal voice trying to communicate with you.

❖ The voice inside you isn't actually a voice whispering in your ears. Rather, it's the thoughts about your experiences. These thoughts are usually so deeply entrenched in the subconscious that you might not even realize you have them.

❖ The inner voice you would encounter might either be self-defeating or affirming. Individuals who have healthy self-esteem normally experience a positive, reassuring inner voice. On the other hand, those who have low self-esteem usually experience an inner voice that is punitive, castigatory, and critical.

❖ For some, documenting is not an easy task, especially if it triggers you to look back at the past traumas that you haven't fully moved on from. If journaling is something too upsetting for you or it gives you a hard time, you can turn to consult a counselor who is able to help you do this exercise easily.

Step 3: Note down your thoughts. The thoughts you're having immediately before your mood changes are a reflection of your inner voice. Known as the "automatic thoughts," they generally reflect how you perceive yourself and everything around you. Documenting these thoughts is going to help you see if a pattern emerges.

- ❖ Automatic thoughts come from the subconscious. That's why sometimes, pinpointing them can be quite challenging. For starters, you can ask yourself, "Why do I feel this way?" Then, you can also dig deeper by asking yourself further questions like "What does it have to do with who I am?" or "Why did I get affected like this?"
- ❖ Usually, the first answers you will get from yourself are pretty superficial ones. That's why you must keep asking, "What else?" until you can probe into your deeper automatic thoughts.
- ❖ For instance, if someone said something offensive, you can write something like, "I find what he said kind of annoying" "I felt angry when he said..." And after asking "What else?" several times, you might eventually identify a thought that you didn't think was there in the

first place, like "I'm more impatient than I think I was."

Step 4: Assess your thought process. After writing down some automatic thoughts, you will start seeing a pattern. Figure out the underlying theme within your thoughts. Are your thoughts healthy and positive or are they self-defeating and negative? Common thought patterns that usually come from negative automatic thoughts include but are not limited to:

❖ All-or-none thinking takes place when you think that one mistake ruins everything. For example, when you make a mistake at your job, you might think that you're a total failure at your job.

❖ Debarring the positive is when you just focus on the bad things you did and completely forget about the positive or good thing you have done. For example, you may focus on the few answers that you got wrong on a test and complete ignore the fact that you've got most answers right.

❖ Jumping to conclusions is when you decide about the things without confirming their authenticity. For example, you might see your friend online on social media so you said hi. You saw him read your message but he didn't reply back right away. So, you automatically assume that he doesn't want to talk to you when in fact, he was just too busy doing something at the moment and was planning to reply back later.

❖ Labeling takes place when someone applies a label to himself or someone else instead of simply acknowledging the behavior or action. For example, rather than thinking, "I could have dealt with that better," you might think, "I am a horrible person."

Step 5: Check your self-esteem. Having healthy self-esteem may reflect your belief that you are worthwhile. Alternatively, if you have low self-esteem, you might feel poorly about yourself and constantly need the approval of other people. If you notice that you're having too many negative thoughts, then you might have low self-esteem. Having low self-esteem carries a negative effect on how you perceive yourself, so it's necessary to intentionally try to have a healthy and balanced perception of who you are as a person. If you are still uncertain whether you are experiencing low self-esteem, then you should become familiar with these three "faces" of negative self-esteem:

- ❖ **The Victim:** This is someone who acts like he is helpless and usually just sit and wait for someone to rescue him. He mastered the art of indifference or self-pity in order to conceal underlying fears of failing. He tends to be unassertive, might be an underachiever, and extremely reliant on other people for hope.

- ❖ **The Imposter:** This is someone who acts as if is happy and everything is going well when he is terrified of failure. The imposter has to always be successful to be happy, usually leading to competition, perfectionism, as well as stress.

- ❖ **The Rebel:** This is someone who constantly tries to downplay others, usually those who are of authority. The rebel tends to be angry all the time about not being good enough and tends to concentrate on not being hurt by the criticism of other people. This may lead to blaming others for his problems, and he may often oppose authority.

Part 2: UNDERSTANDING YOUR PERSONALITY TYPE

Get a piece of paper and place it in front of you. Make sure that the paper is in a vertical position. Place is on a hard surface so you can write on it easily.

On the paper, draw five lines vertically. These lines will create boxes which give you spaces to write, so see to it that there's enough space in between these lines.

In each space, write each following word: "Agreeableness," "Neuroticism," "Extraversion," "Conscientiousness," and "Openness to Experience." These words are the "The Big Five" personality traits. Based on many studies, these five personality traits show the general components of human personality that are most essential in interpersonal communications.

❖ Remember that these "Big Five" qualities aren't personality types but parts of the personality. For example, you might be high in "Agreeableness" or friendliness but pretty low with "Extraversion" or sociability. It's possible for someone to be very friendly but at the same time, not be very social.

❖ The "Emotional Stability" can also be referred to as the "Neuroticism" characteristic.

❖ In the same way, "Openness to Experience" can sometimes be referred to as "Intellect."

Figure out where you are on all the five dimensions. It's common for people to mostly fall in the high spectrum or the low spectrum of every personality dimension. Take some time to consider where you really belong. Put "High" or "Low" in every corresponding box that you made. Below are descriptions of every trait in order to guide you with your self-assessment:

❖ Extroversion is a reflection of a keen interest in other people as well as external events. People that are very extroverted tend to have more confidence and don't have any problem exploring unexplored territories. On the other hand, those who are low in extroversion are usually referred to as "introverts" and tend to isolate themselves and enjoy quiet environments.

❖ Neuroticism refers to the anxiety level. Those who are high in this dimension generally experience negative emotions, which are usually stronger compared to their counterparts. If you're always worrying and always seem to be freaking out, then you're probably high in this area.

❖ Openness to Experience specifies how willing you are to adjust your thinking when something new arises. A person who is high in this area is someone who is probably eccentric and free-spirited. If you happen to be low in this area, then chances are, you are more conventional and tangible with your thinking patterns.

❖ Conscientiousness is how much you consider other people every time you need to make a decision. This also reflects your level of self-control. If you happen to be high in this area, then you're probably well-organized, efficient, and function properly with independence. If you happen to be low in this area, then you might be spontaneous and impulsive and do well in places and situations that are always changing.

❖ Agreeableness specifies the level to which someone is compatible with other people. This also shows how much someone cares about other people. If you happen to be high in this area, then chances are, you're pretty empathetic and it's so easy for you to relate to and understand others. People might describe you as "nice" and "kind-hearted." On the other hand, if you are low in this area, then you don't put a lot of emphasis on your and other people's emotions when making any form of actions.

Ponder how these traits affect your personality. It's human nature for us to exhibit behavior and choose environments depending on what we feel is comfortable for our personality. This self-assessment exercise might provide you with a great understanding of why you act or think a certain way.

Part 3: WRITING A SELF-ASSESSMENT FOR WORK

Pick the right time. Make sure to save some time for this exercise as this quick self-reflection can be really beneficial for you. During this time, you will want to concentrate on your goals, habits, competencies, as well as overall performance. Simply spending an hour to review personal notes and other details is going to help you write a precise self-evaluation of how you do see yourself.

Write down your accomplishments from your workplace throughout the past year. You don't have to be shy about writing all the things you achieved – you worked hard for them. There's nothing wrong about being proud of yourself. The main purpose of self-analysis is to highlight all of your accomplishments. Think of all of the projects that you have done, extra responsibilities that you performed, and all the hard work you did just to benefit the company you are working for. When it's possible, use these specific examples throughout your self-assessment.

❖ You can check back on your previous emails in order for you to remember some of your accomplishments that you might have already forgotten.

❖ If you have a folder on your computer where you save all your previous assignments, check it out to see if you have documents that will remind you of your previous achievements.

Document the areas that you'd want to improve on. It's so tempting to only focus on your accomplishments. However, pinpointing the areas you need improvements in is very important when it comes to self-analysis. Consider areas you wish you were better in to attain your goals more efficiently. When you reflect your challenges as well, you are able to get a more precise reflection of your actual performance.

Make a list of goals that you'd want to accomplish in the following year. This would be your action plan, and you must concentrate on things that you are able to do to improve your performance at work. See to it that the goals evidently show your commitment to giving more value to your workplace.

Part 4: MEASURING YOUR LEVEL OF STRESS

Recall any life changes that happened to you recently. Good changes and bad changes happen and become normal in an adult's life. Some of the good changes include getting a higher paying job, moving to a new house, getting a promotion, or getting married, while the bad ones include being laid off, losing someone close to you, breakup, etc. You have to remember that any kind of change can be pretty stressful as you will need to make some sort of adjustment. Take your time to consider and list down all the changes that you might have experienced in the last few months that might have caused you stress and pain.

Dwell on your values. When you live a life that contradicts with your values and beliefs, then expect to experience a high level of stress. For instance, if you're someone who is very ambitious and competitive, but you are stuck in a dull dead-end job, then this life that is not aligned will also cause you a great amount of stress. If your values and belief systems don't match your actual life experience, you might have a life that is filled with stress and discontentment. Here are important questions you should ask yourself in order to identify if there are any mismatches in your life that causes you stress:

❖ What values in life do you give importance to? Success? Family? Hobbies? Kindness? Religious beliefs?

❖ Do your actions and lifestyle conflict with these values? For example, say one of your values is making your family happy. Do you really spend enough time with them to make them happy?

❖ Do your hobbies, job, relationships, or other aspects of your life conflict with these values?

See the things around you. The places you go and the things you do – how much do they contribute to the stress levels you have to deal with? If you are living in a place that is surrounded by crime, pollution, trash, or any other unpleasant elements, then you are also likely dealing with stress a lot. Figure out the source of stress.

Think about your personal issues and social dynamics. Personal issues and social factors can have a great effect on your stress level. Below are some aspects to consider when you're trying to assess how these features are affecting your stress level:

❖ Finances: Do you have enough funds to afford your basic and daily needs?

❖ Family: Is everyone in the family alright and in a good situation?

❖ Health: Is your health and that of your family in a good condition?

Monitor your sleep. Not getting enough sleep can highly affect a lot of areas of your life, which of course can boost the levels of your stress. Track the length of your sleep every night. Even though the amount of sleep that one needs varies from person to person, the average duration of sleep should be 6 to 8 hours and many adults have a hard time attaining those numbers.

Because of this, your stress levels might be higher compared to people who get enough sleep. Here are the areas of your life that can be affected by lack of sleep:

❖ Your thinking process

❖ Difficulty in focusing

❖ Health problems, including a high risk of chronic diseases

❖ Forgetfulness

❖ Lower libido

❖ Early aging

❖ Weight gain

Think of the ways how you can manage your stress. List down all the things that you are able to do in order to improve your life. After all, the main objective of self-analysis is to promote growth in your life.

How does this help you analyze others?

Being able to understand yourself better can also help you improve your capacity to better understand other people's thoughts and emotions.

A German study suggests that those who participated in a psychology-training program to improve their "perspective-taking", which is a term used by psychologists to describe the ability to know the "inner world" of another person became better at analyzing themselves and analyzing others. The term inner world means a person's beliefs, thoughts, emotions, and personality.

One study published in the Journal of Cognitive Enhancement shows there's some truth to the saying that, "In order to know someone, you must know yourself first."

Knowing yourself completely at a deeper level isn't simply just to boost your ego. When you know yourself better, it's going to be easier for you to view yourself from another person's perspective. It is also going to be useful in improving your social skills.

Looking Inward

There was a study where researchers looked into data gathered from two groups of approximately 80 adults each who were all living in Germany and were between the ages of 20 and 55.

The study consisted of a 3-day retreat followed by a 2-hour meeting every week throughout the following 3 months. The people who participated were trained to develop skills to help them improve their inner awareness. Some of the skills they tried to develop were how to keep doing meditation exercise regularly wherein they observed the thoughts that came up into their heads without being emotionally involved.

This exercise was designed to help the participants get more understanding of how their minds work without reacting too much to it.

Some other skills that were assigned involved improving their "inner parts" that were related to their own psyche, such as optimism, judgment, management, etc.

The participants were asked to observe the "inner parts" that would be stimulated within themselves in daily situations, like every time they are at work, when they are playing with their kids, or other things that you usually do within the day.

Throughout one session, the participants worked in pairs in order to complete an exercise wherein one of them acted as a speaker and chose a recent situation that happened to him but described it from the standpoint of one of their inner parts. Throughout the exercise, a participant listened and tried to guess the speaker's inner parts that the speaker was trying to portray. This is an activity that improves perspective-taking or understanding the thoughts of other people.

By performing this exercise on a regular basis, one can detach from the inner parts that are routinely stimulated in certain circumstances. This lets them be more flexible when it comes to their typical behavior patterns.

Understanding others

Based on the study, the more participants recognized these internal characteristics of personality, the better they understood other people's intentions and beliefs.

Fascinatingly, the research found that those who could recognize more negative inner parts of personality were more likely to have improvements in analyzing others. It was kind of astounding that being able to recognize positive inner parts wasn't associated with a better analysis of other people. It looks like that in most participants, being able to recognize the negative inner parts was what really improved skills and dedication.

In order to face your own negative inner parts, you might have to go through your inner resistance against some painful emotions, so maybe that is the reason why people who faced these parts had a better understanding of other people.

Even though not everyone might have access to the form of training used in this research, there are many other ways to acquire similar skills and understanding.

Mindfulness training, meditation, and other forms of self-inquiry could all be great experiences.

1.2 How to Understand Your Thoughts, Behaviors, and Actions

According to Science, our thoughts on everything that happens to us can have a huge effect on the way we feel. I'm not only talking about the big things that happen to us but even the smallest issues. However, our thinking is not always accurate or obvious. If you become more familiar with our thinking patterns, you will have more understanding with others.

It's so easy to believe that every time something bad happen to us, we use it as our foundation for what we feel and our decisions. However, studies have shown that it's not really the event itself that triggers our emotional reaction. Instead, it is the automatic thoughts that go through our head in instant response to the event. However, our emotional reaction could be so fast that our thoughts are not very obvious.

While our thoughts and emotional responses will be appropriate in most occasions, there might still be times that they will not. If you happen to have inappropriate thoughts, especially in reaction to negative events, they are able to drive stronger reactions and emotions than needed. Furthermore, we can fall into patterns that could be harmful to our happiness not only temporarily but also in the longer term.

There have been proofs that suggest that if we can become good at recognizing our thoughts when it comes to things that happen and when these are not accurate, we can become better at analyzing and managing our emotional reactions.

This might have a great effect on our own happiness and also on our interactions with the people we work or live with.

Getting Started

1. Breaking things down into ABC

The first thing you have to do is to learn how you can unravel your feelings, thoughts, and actions.

One of the founders of cognitive behavioral therapy, Dr. Albert Ellis, developed what's usually known the A-B-C model that is a great way to separate things out.

The letter **A** stands for **A**ctivating Event, which refers to the things that have taken place; B stands for **B**elief, which are the thoughts that directly come up in our head; and **C** is for **C**onsequences, which are the emotions we have and how we are reacting consequently.

Dr. Ellis found that the way people interpret things that are taking place in their lives and the things they say to themselves (B) play a big part in how they feel emotionally and how they behave (C).

Below are examples that show how people thinking differently about the same event can affect people's feelings and behaviors differently.

Example #1: **A**ctivating event

You're grinding hard for an upcoming deadline. Your boss asks you multiple times that week about the report and reminds you that he wants to see it first before it goes to the client.

Person 1:

Belief - "My boss doesn't trust me and that I'm incapable of doing this by myself. He thinks that I'm just messing around not doing it."

Consequences — He feels worried, pressured, and stressed. He has a hard time concentrating on the report and makes mistakes. He has trouble sleeping.

Person 2:

Belief - "YES! This project is very important and thankfully, my boss keeps checking in and that he wants to read it to make sure that it will be okay with the client."

Consequences - He feels calmed and supported. He continues working on the report, excited to show the result to the boss.

Example 2: **A**ctivating event

You're having a bad day. Walking home, you saw your friend a few meters away walking toward the other direction. You wave at him and it seems like he just ignored you.

Person 1:

Belief - "I can't believe he just ignored me. I might have done something that made him upset. Or perhaps, he just doesn't want to talk to me at all."

Consequences - He feels upset and down, not bothering to call or text his friend anymore. He stays inside and prefers not to talk with anyone.

Person2:

Belief – "He looked so distracted, and he didn't even notice me. I hope he's fine."

Consequences - He feels alright, pretty worried about the friend. He calls his friend to see if he's okay.

So, which one are you, the Person 1 or the Person 2?

2. Challenging your thoughts

For most of us, tuning into our thoughts or beliefs is something that is not easy. Most of the time, an event is going to activate some sort of emotional response in us that is going to affect our behavior. Usually, unless we take a minute and do some reflection, we are either unconscious of our thoughts with regard to the event that generated the emotion, or we leave our interpretation unopposed.

Of course, it might be that our interpretations are right and the way we feel and act in response is suitable. But by tuning into the things, we tell ourselves to think more thoroughly and carefully. We let ourselves be challenged by those thoughts that are illogical or harmful by asking ourselves questions like:

- ❖ What proofs do we have that says our thoughts are true?
- ❖ What could be the other reasons why this happened?
- ❖ Is thinking the way I currently do would help the situation?
- ❖ If my thoughts are correct, what can I do to fix the issue?

By asking yourself the logical questions, you can prevent yourself from getting into bad or negative places. It allows you to hold the fort of how you choose to react.

In Example 2 mentioned above, the Person 1 could have challenged himself by asking what proof he has that he has done something bad that upset his friend – maybe the friend was rushing to do something to even notice you or that he was not wearing his eyeglasses. If he thinks these thoughts, then he could save himself from feeling down and becoming worried.

When something makes you feel upset or worried, or when anything gives you negative feelings, try this ABC exercise on yourself. And if you make it a habit, you will see how it can make your life happier and less stressful.

3. Finding the patterns

By becoming adapted at tuning in to the way you look at things and interpret events, you may begin to notice that you say the same things to yourself time and again.

Maybe, you're someone who constantly blames himself or constantly blames other people when things go bad or someone who believes they're not doing good enough and other people are better than them. Maybe you're prone to worrying about things all the time – even though those things may not, and often don't, happen.

As you can see in the ABC example mentioned above, every means of interpreting an event has an effect on our actions and emotions. If we develop a specific obstructive pattern of thoughts, it's possible that certain emotions will also become accustomed to us. For instance, people who blame themselves are more likely to experience feelings of guilt or sadness, while those who tend to blame other people will feel angrier. Those who feel they are not good enough are likely to feel sad or shameful.

1.3 Understanding Other People's Traits and Flaws

It's generally a good idea to hold yourself to high standards and go all-out. But there are times when people have unrealistic beliefs when it comes to things that they are capable of and should do. The standards they set are impractically high. Then if they make a mistake, they might get too disappointed and unforgiving to themselves. That is a bad form of *perfectionism*. This is when someone sees as unacceptable anything but being perfect. These feelings can increase stress and bring about signs of depression.

However, self-compassion could help you protect yourself from such negative impacts. Self-compassion can be described as treating yourself how you would describe your best friend.

When things go wrong, it's so easy to say good things to other people to console them. However, it's even easier to choose to be mean to yourself. But even if it's the case, many of us still can't still understand people.

A lot of us complain about others, usually about people who do the same thing over and over again. I must admit, I used to be that person who complains a lot about others. Some of the things you would hear from me included:

- ❖ He's so annoying.
- ❖ I hate it when people are always late; why can't they respect other people's time?!
- ❖ I would never do that to anyone. He's such a horrible person for even thinking about that!
- ❖ Our neighbors are always fighting;, sometimes it keeps me up all night because I can hear them arguing.
- ❖ It's so disgusting how some people would leave dirty dishes and not wash them right away.

But now, I came to a realization that I don't have to like other people and they don't have to change because of me. All I can do is to accept them with their flaws and who they are as a person. It's all up to me how I am going to deal with them. I mean, I can criticize them all day long, but at the end of the day, it's their life and they are the only ones to deal with it.

This is what I call Reality Training, which is recognizing that if you don't have a happier life, then you must learn how to accept people as they are and look for ways how you can deal with them, or just completely get them out of the picture.

It's all up to you whether or not you want to tolerate them or simply walk away from them because of their traits that you don't like. *That's the reality of it!* The truth is, you will only have two options; it's either you stop dealing with the person completely, or accept that person and adjust to how they are. Trying to change the person is not the best option because first of all, it's not always effective, and secondly, imagine someone trying to change you... would you like it? Voluntarily changing how you react to that person's flaws would be one of the best choices.

Not everyone will change just because you said so. That's why if you want to fix the situation, you're the one who needs to control your reaction. When I recognized this, I was still in the early phase of my marriage. It really drove me insane whenever my wife would tell me that she wants to watch a movie with me in bed. She would fall asleep within the next 15 minutes in the movie – I complained about it whenever she did it.

She kept telling me that she was just tired but she didn't mean to piss me off or anything. I then realized that she's right; she meant well. So, every time she asks for movies, I just let her sleep. I still finished the movies and even turned the volume low so she could sleep better. I accepted this thing about her that I initially thought was annoying, and I'm sure she did accept the things about me that she might have found annoying as well – I'm not perfect. I try to consider things and accept things about her to avoid pointless arguments and to make her happy and it worked; many things that I found annoying no longer affect me.

Adjust your expectations.

What you might think wrong might not look wrong to others. If you feel like something is unacceptable, handle it in a different way. Being self-righteous over something that you disagree with triggers needless stress. Giving someone sermons about good behavior usually does nothing.

Once I learned this reality, I told my colleague who used to annoy me all the time by being late, "Meet me at this restaurant. I will already order my appetizer, so I can eat while waiting." Then I have a friend who would bail out the last minute before the meet up we agreed. So, I did the same thing once. He got a little frustrated. I told him I just couldn't take him seriously because he always cancelled the last minute. He apologized and said he would not do it again, and to this day, he always kept his promise. All because I decided to change how I respond to the situations! Sometimes, people give better response to actions than complaints.

Here are some circumstances that portray common realities:

Reality: *Parents usually see things differently because they stick to older values.*

Having an argument with parents can be really frustrating. Because they grew up with different values, they are not as open-minded as today's generation. For many of them, if they don't understand what you are doing, then you're probably wrong. Instead of arguing with them, it's better to work with that reality. Accept the fact that no matter how much you explain things to them, they'll never get them. Forcing them to understand things would be unnecessary. You don't have to bother. And because your parents wouldn't change their thoughts about it, you can simply change your ways instead. You can tell them that they might not understand you, but it's okay. Assure them that nothing's wrong with what you are doing or thinking and there's no point arguing about it.

Reality: *We might have friends that have annoying traits.*

If you are friends with someone you like hanging out with but they are always late, instead of being annoyed that they are always late, you can change your response. It is your choice to be friends and make a plan with someone who you know might keep you waiting all the time. If you know he's always late, then why don't you arrive late or set the time of the meeting earlier?

If you have a friend who talks a lot, try to accept that it's a part of his personality. After all, it's better to have a talkative friend than having someone next to you who just nods and say nothing.

If your friend would always invite to see you but bail out the last minute, then the next time he calls to see you, tell him you're the one who would call and tell him when you're not busy anymore.

If you have a friend who would borrow money and would not pay you within the promised timeframe, then you must remind yourself that it was never your obligation to lend him money, so next time he asks, refuse.

If you raised the issue to someone but they still kept doing what they were doing, then it's time to give up.

You have to do what you have to do. If their behavior bothers you, avoid the situation to get to that point. You know what they say, prevention is better than cure!

CHAPTER 2

ANALYZING OTHERS

First of all, before analyzing someone, there's one question you need to answer…

"Why do I need to analyze this person?"

You need to perform analysis about another person normally tells you the type of analysis that has to be performed. If someone's applying for a job, then a certain type of analysis is used. On the other hand, if you are performing analysis on someone for mental disturbance, then another set of procedures has to be used.

Once you have answered the question as to why you must do it, then you can then proceed. Now, let's assume that you are evaluating someone for a job application.

Then the next question you have to figure out the answer to is, what are the strengths of the person?

However, of course, the right answer will usually depend on the strengths that are necessary for the position. In this as well, we usually have to follow the needs of the assessment. If you think that leadership skills would be necessary, then you may want to focus on finding "sociability" and "dominant" traits.

After learning the applicant's strengths, the next thing you need to be aware of is his weaknesses. You have to know the traits that may affect the person's performance negatively. Can they be considered as impulsive, easily distracted, or easily pressured?

Having a general list is useful since it usually highlights problems and traits that weren't initially considered. In this sense, your analysis normally starts with a screening for the most common general traits and a screening for psychopathology.

2.1 What Does Analyzing Someone Involve?

While it's impossible to read someone's innermost feelings and thoughts, there is still another way to read someone, and that is through his body language. On top of that, a person's eyes are usually very communicative as well.

This reminds me of the time I met this guy called Dan at the gym. I mean, we never really had an actual conversation, but I noticed how he came at the gym every day at the same time. I know this sounds like a pretty insignificant detail for a lot of people, but for someone who knows how to analyze people, this detail meant a lot.

Dan was self-motivated, determined, organized, and very consistent with his goals. These traits became obvious to me only because I noticed how punctual he was.

But aside from that, there are other things that I noticed about this guy. He would wear tank tops that showed his muscular physique, and he would do exercises that are not normally done by most people in the gym. This made me think that he's a guy who loved showing up.

When doing further analysis, I figured out that he's an only child in the family.

When you are analyzing someone's personality, you have to keep in mind that the person's birth order plays a part in his personality. Most of the time, children that have no siblings are showered with attention growing up and that is the reason why even when they grow old, they still crave for attention.

The guy loved wearing black; he would wear black all the time, even after his work out – especially after work out, actually. When he took out his phone from his pocket, its cover was also black. Even the car he drove was black.

When analyzing the personality of someone, you should understand that people may go too extreme when they want to escape from something. Coming to the gym regularly and wearing black showed that the guy wanted to look tough and strong.

When I gathered further information, I learned that my assumptions were true. When the guy was still a little kid, he used to be bullied at school, and he felt like he was a weak person. That's why when he grew up, he promised to not appear weak. He started going to the gym regularly and wore black all the time to cover and run away from his past.

Another aspect you have to consider when analyzing the personality of a person is that connecting the dots must always initiate with a straight line. So, what does it mean? Well, it means that if my speculations were true, then definitely, we must expect to find that he's doing other activities that were able to help him become stronger apart from coming to the gym.

And my guess was true; Dan was also doing martial arts.

Here are some tips for you to get started:

Be Objective

You must to go at it without prejudice or being biased. There's undeniably no point in "objectively" doing your best analyzing someone if you've already had a stereotype for them. You have to get rid of all the layers of prejudice in order for you to see beyond your first impression.

Look at Non-verbal Signs

Your approach to analyzing someone must be a combination of being steered by your intuition, emotional intelligence, as well as observing the person's behavior and physical movements.

Most of the time, people would lean their body in the direction of something they like and lean away from something that makes them angry or uncomfortable. The same thing goes for which directions the person's toes are pointed. If they're pointing their body and feet right at you, it's possibly a sign that they're comfortable with you or want to talk to you.

Is someone biting his nails? This could be an indication that the person might be feeling anxious or nervous. This is something that is extremely common for people who are under pressure.

Other signs of someone feeling tension might be seen in facial expressions. Grinding of teeth, gritting of teeth, and puckered lips might show that they're feeling upset and are trying to inhibit what they're wanting to say.

What's the posture telling you?

It's not difficult to notice confidence in a person by simply looking at how someone carries himself. If you see them cowering or slouching, it might be a sign that they might have low self-esteem. You will see a clear line between a posture that radiates confidence and the exaggerated swagger that goes with an inflated ego.

Create a baseline

Most of us carry some sort of behavioral quirks. Sometimes, these behavior patterns are habitual. Some of these quirks include scratching of head, clearing their throat before they talk, looking at the floor, and fondling the back of their necks. You have to read what the "normal" behavior of the person is. That's going to be your baseline. It's not a good thing to overanalyze that someone is feeling nervous or telling a lie only because you saw them biting their fingernails. Nail biting is a known mannerism for many, so it could be something normal. So, make sure to take that in consideration.

Look for Clusters

The moment you've established a baseline for the person you're talking to, search for clusters of behavior that are not included in the baseline. Did you notice any sort of contradiction between their physical gestures and their normal behavior?

Another thing that can help you point out a baseline inconsistency is Phoneme awareness. This is a basic component of phonetic speech. If a person is feeling extremely nervous or is lying, you might notice how their voice might raise or lower. They may overstress certain words as overcompensation in order to manipulate you to make you believe them.

It doesn't mean that because someone has a very loud voice, he's the strongest person in the room. Although people with loud, big voice might be intimidating, having a loud voice might just indicate someone's confidence. Unless of course if you're dealing with someone who manipulates with a personality issue. Sociopaths or psychopaths are usually hard to read since people cannot see past their charm.

Consider Context

While it's true that crossed arms might be an indication that someone's closing himself off because he might not feel comfortable in the situation he is in, but it's also possible that he's just feeling cold. It's important to be observant in order to broaden your field of focus and also not to get preoccupied with one tell-tale sign.

Understand Your Intuition

It's important to trust your gut. It's important that you open yourself up to their vibe and try to make sense of the emotions and feelings a person induces in you. Natural instinct plays a big part in our daily life, so it's very important. This is not about trying to read someone's aura. It's about reading how one's body and mind work to their presence every time they have an encounter.

Bottom Line

Analyzing people isn't just about protecting ourselves from prospective liars and scammers. The main goal for learning how to analyze someone isn't to train yourself to be a criminal profiler. The goal of this is to improve your observation skills in order for you to make better decisions in your life. Being able to analyze people we're working with or interacting with can help a great deal in our lives.

Why learn to do this? What are the benefits?

Why do you think that we tend to get along so well with some people while there are some people that we just can't manage to be with? Why is that there are times it's so easy to predict how someone will react to a certain situation? Well, there's a big chance that it has to do with that person's personality type preference.

The truth is, each of us has a specific preference that makes up our type of personality and it just happens that some personalities work better together than others.

Chances are, your personality might work so well with one person and might not work so well with another.

A person's type of personality, together with his opinions, work ethics, as well as attitude, plays a part in making it easy or hard to get along with others. However, when you are aware of your own personality, it's going to be easier for you to observe and adapt to other people and even the situation around you. With this awareness, you will be able to learn not only about yourself but also about others.

The Myers-Briggs Personality Type Indicator, which we will talk about further later in this book, gives a great detailed analysis into the main personality preferences and leanings a person has – it goes deeper on the differences between thinking and feeling, introversion and extraversion, intuition and sensing, etc.

But then again, this kind of assessment is not necessary to be able to truly understand yourself and other people around you. By becoming more self-aware and having acceptance for those people around you, no matter how different they are from you, you will be able to reap these benefits:

You will be aware of your preferences. Each person has their own psychological type inclinations and working within these inclinations usually lets us be most effective, efficient, and our most comfortable with ourselves. On the other hand, working beyond these limits will require you more time and energy and normally leads to lower quality work. Being aware of these boundaries — and knowing when you are within or beyond them —helps you improve your efficiency, productivity, and time management skills.

You can avoid conflict. By being mindful of other people's personality, you can prevent conflicts. If you know how other people may have a tendency to be impulsive whenever something comes up, it becomes easier for you to adjust your reaction.

You can appreciate diversity. Recognizing how your personality type differs from and interacts with other types can provide you with a great appreciation for people's differences and what it offers to your life. Sometimes, it is just really nice to have that very creative mind that helps you create ideas that only certain minds can come up with.

You can choose the right people. A big part of being an adult is the necessity to choose which ones to keep and which ones to avoid. As adults, we want to get rid of those who bring toxic vibes in our lives and make it more difficult than it already is. And the first step to know which ones you need in your life is to learn about their personalities.

The concept behind personality type is that it's something we are born with, live with, as well as die with. It is something that develops and evolves over time. It is up to us how we use it or apply it differently based on our experiences. However, it is something that normally stays the same our whole life. By entirely understanding personality types of each person you interact with, you are able to learn to appreciate their strong points and also recognize and accept their weaknesses. On top of it, you also learn your capacity to accept people for who they are.

2.2 How to analyze someone using effective techniques

As a psychiatrist, it is part of my job to read people, not only based on what they say but also who they are as a person. It is my job to interpret their verbal and nonverbal cues to learn what kind of people they are. Logic alone is not enough to learn a person's whole story. It is necessary to surrender other vital kinds of information in order to learn how to read the necessary non-verbal instinctive cues that people radiate. In order to do this, you should also be willing to submit to any biases or emotional baggage like old hatreds or ego clashes that holds you back from seeing someone's personality and characters clearly. The key is to stay objective and get information impartially without misrepresenting it.

Whether you are trying to read your friend, co-worker, or partner in order to understand them exactly, it's important to surrender biases, and all kinds of walls should be destroyed. You need to be ready to get rid of old, restrictive ideas you might have. Those people who can read other people well are skilled to read the invisible. They have learned to use what I like to call the "super-senses" to look beyond where you normally put your attention in order to access life-changing instinctive visions.

Three Techniques to Analyze People

1. Reading the Body Language

Studies have shown that words account for just 7% of how people communicate while our body language gives off 55% and the tone of our voice tone about 30%. Here, a vital point to keep in mind is that you are not trying too hard to read someone's body language. It wouldn't help to be too analytical. Just stay relaxed and adaptable. Stay comfortable, relax, and just observe.

> Observe the Appearance

Before fully reading a person's body language, here is something you might want to notice first: What do they wear? Are they wearing refined, suited up clothing or are they just wearing relaxed jeans and shirt preferring to look and feel all casual? Are they wearing revealing clothing that show up too much skin? Or perhaps they are wearing accessories that represent their spiritual or religious beliefs? Most of the time, how a person represents himself based on his clothing says a lot about his personality.

> Look at the Body Posture

Here is something you must ask yourself when reading someone's body posture: Do they always hold their heads high looking all confident? Or do you notice them walk irresolutely or shy away, which can be a sign of having low self-esteem? Do they carry themselves with a chest all puffed out, which can be a sign of having a huge ego?

> Notice the Physical Movements

❖ *Leaning and distance* – Check out where they lean. Normally, we lean toward the things that we like and try to stay away from the ones we don't.

❖ *Crossed legs and arms* – These poses may suggest being angry, defensive, or protective. When you see someone crossing their legs, they tend to point their foot toward someone they feel comfortable with.

❖ *Hiding of hands* – When you see someone put their hands in their pockets, laps, or just anywhere they can't be seen, it may suggest that they are not very comfortable.

❖ *Cuticle picking or biting of lips* – When you notice someone biting or licking their lips or picking their cuticles, it might be their way of soothing themselves under a situation that makes them feel awkward or pressurized.

> Understand Facial Expressions

Feelings can become imprinted on our facial expressions, and this is definitely the easiest thing to learn how to read. When you see someone's face with deep frown lines, that may suggest overthinking or feeling worried. On the other hand, crow's feet indicate smile lines of joy. When you see someone with pursed lips, it is probably a sign of anger, bitterness, or contempt. You'll know someone is angry when you notice him with a clenched jaw and grinding teeth.

2. Listen to Your Intuition

You are able to tune into someone further than their words and body language. Intuition is what you feel in your guts and not what you hear your head say. It is the nonverbal details that you see through pictures and ah-has, instead of logic. If you would like to truly get to understand someone, the most important thing you must understand is who the person is from the inside, and not who they seem like from the outside. Intuition allows you to see beyond the obvious to tell you more about the story.

Intuitive Cues Checklist

✓ *Acknowledge your gut feelings*

Feel your guts and honor it, especially the first time you meet someone; it's an intuitive reaction that takes place before having a chance to think. It conveys whether you feel comfortable or not. Gut feelings take place in an instant – it's a primal, immediate response. They are your inner truth pattern, which relays if you are able to trust people.

✓ *Don't ignore the goosebumps*

Goosebumps are spectacular intuitive stings that say that we resound with people who affect us or are saying something that moves us. We also get goosebumps whenever we experience Deja-vu, which is a recognition that we experience during the time we feel like we've already known or experienced something.

✓ *Heed the flashes of insight*

During normal conversations, you might get an "ah-ha" about those who come out of the blue. Be alert. Otherwise, you'll probably be going to miss it. Sometimes, we just tend to go onto the next thought so quickly that we lose critical insights immediately.

✓ *Be aware of intuitive empathy*

Sometimes you are able to feel emotions in your body and even physical symptoms of other people which can be considered as a strong form of empathy. So, when you're trying to analyze someone, try to notice: "Do I feel down when I was talking to him? Does it make me feel heavy when I'm around him?"

3. Sense the Emotional Energy

Human emotions are a great expression of our energy; this is what we like to call the "vibe". We use it together with intuition. There are some people who we feel good to be around; you know, those people who can easily improve our vitality and mood. On the other hand, there are people who are just so draining; the ones we immediately want to avoid as soon as we feel their presence. This is a "subtle energy" that we can feel inches or feet away from the body even if we don't feel them visually. In Chinese medicine, this is what they called the *chi,* an essential vitality that plays a part in a human's overall wellbeing.

Strategies to Read Emotional Energy

1. Sense the presence of others

This is the energy that we are emitting, not essentially corresponding with our behavior or words. It is the emotional atmosphere that goes around us such as a drizzled rain and ray of sunshine. When trying to read or analyze someone, ask this question: Do you feel a friendly presence around them? Or seeing them makes you want to avoid them?

2. Look them in the eyes

Our eyes are the most expressive part of the body, and they are good at transmitting powerful energy. Just like how our brain has an electromagnetic sign that extends beyond the body, research shows that our eyes can project this as well. As much as possible, you want to take time observing people's eyes. Are they lazy? Reclusive? Outgoing? Approachable? Bored? Angry?

3. Notice the way they interact

As humans, we like sharing emotional energy with physical contact, and it goes throughout like an electrical current. Whenever you make interactions like hugging, handshaking, or even by simply tapping, ask yourself, does it make you feel warm? Do the way they do it feels confident or comfortable? Or does it put you off? Is the person's hand shaky, which indicates nervousness or anxiety? Or does it feel like they are simply forced to do those interactions?

4. Listen for the tone of their reaction

The way someone talks – through tone and volume – can tell so much about a person's emotions. The frequencies of the sound generate vibrations. When you read people, notice how the tone of their voice makes you feel. Ask yourself: Does it feel soothing? Snippy? Sarcastic? Abrasive?

2.3 How to Tell If Someone Has A Bad Character or Good Character

In order to best identify if someone has a bad or good character, you must answer this question clearly first: What do you consider a good and a bad character?

There are a lot of different opinions when it comes to what's good and bad traits. There are a lot of popular traits that most of us consider good or bad, but all in all, it's subjective and it all depends on you.

Even though you'd know the most common traits, you'd still be averaging those characteristics and again, you'd need to choose which of the many possibilities you agree on.

Take your time to list down all the pros and cons of having different character traits. From the list you make, write the ones you think are good and bad. Now, when analyzing someone, find what traits they have that belong to the good and bad lists you made. However, you must keep in mind that to know a person's traits, you might need to get to know them a little longer than just basing it on the first impression. Otherwise, your chance of being wrong is high.

The more we spend time to get to know someone, the more we understand why they act a certain way and the more it becomes easy for us to accept them. Once you start to accept someone for the traits they have, you might start seeing those traits as not bad ones.

Overall, a good or bad character is still based on what you think it is. When it comes to what others think of you, asking them is the best way to find out. And yes, while finding out the difference between good and bad traits can be a long process, it is worth the energy and time you put in.

If you want a shortcut, then follow your instinct and don't judge people. You just use your instinct to guide you on who to avoid and who to keep around. Judging is biased and not at all reliable. When it comes to fully getting to know a person, it's almost impossible to do that no matter how long you've known that person; it is only that person who knows who he truly is.

Analyzing Someone Based on How He Treats Others

The most important relationship you will have in your life is the relationship you will have with yourself. This is not to say that other relationships shouldn't matter that much. However, at the end of the day, no one cares about you more than you do.

Every person wants to be liked and accepted by others. Fitting in with others is human nature. When you act instinctively without being thinking about your intentions, you're performing unconscious commands.

This is why it's easy to read someone's personality based on how they treat others.

If someone treats people or you badly by being either rude, uncompassionate, insensitive, disrespectful, violent, they are extremely unreliable or untrustworthy; They might tell many lies or just spread gossips; you would want to steer clear of those people in your life. You are able to judge for yourself based on the way a person behaves towards other people. Allow your instincts to do the job of deciding things for you. They're already judging others, and there's a big possibility that they are also judging you. Admit it, there were probably times when you quietly judged people who you know judge others or treat other people like crap. They treat most people badly, there is then a recurring pattern developing. If I see someone treat others badly, I keep myself aware of it and I try not to deal with them at all costs.

On the other hand, when someone is nice to other people, it's so easy to assume that they are great people. We love to be around them, and in return, it's so easy to be nice to them. After all, the saying that "treat others the way they treat you" is so easy to follow. But what if they only do that to look good because they have negative intentions? Perhaps they use this attitude to mask their real personality.

But then again, this is only one way to analyze someone. It's still important to take information from multiple different perspectives and use your logic by considering possible scenarios as to why a person would respond or act this way and saving actual judgment until you're extremely sure rather than simply passing judgment irrationally and without cause.

For example, maybe someone is mean to another person because that person did something awful to him, but the reality is that he is the nicest person you'd ever meet. Similarly, someone might initially show up as the nicest person but when we're not looking, they are just simply horrible.

All in all, even though analyzing someone based on how they treat people is effective most of the time, other times, that's not who they are, and there's a deeper reason as to why they act a certain way toward others. It would be a great idea to observe and consider other possibilities instead of committing to a certain action or thought inconsiderately or foolishly.

2.4 How to Analyze Someone Through Their Environment

Identifying confidence & insecurity

- **How to differentiate**

In the society we have today, it seems like confidence is usually seen as a sign of being independent, strong, and even being smart. On the contrary of that is insecurity, which might have seen as being timid, shy, and even anti-social. Insecurity manifests itself in a person by holding them back in life due to fear. This is where the battle of insecurity against confidence starts.

Yes, these usually are the first impressions on these two different personalities. However, it's always beyond that. Actually, the entire picture will look different based on your unique situation. Each person has their own strengths, weaknesses, challenges, and achievements. We tend to feel confident and insecure in certain situations.

We can only hope for confidence to rule our lives rather than our insecurities. One of the best places to start when trying to work on our confidence is to know where we are.

Ask yourself… which one currently prevails in your life, your confidence or your insecurity? If your friends will describe you, how do you think they will?

Open to Learning vs. Fear of Changing

The moment you open yourself to changing and embrace the possibility of acquiring the lessons and experiences – whether good and bad – you are showing a sign of confidence. You don't fear to fail since you trust yourself as well as your skills.

Accepting any forms of lessons as they come is a very powerful way to develop your confidence. The more you accept that it's okay to commit mistakes, the more you open yourself to take advice from others, and the more willing you are to take risks, the more confident you will be about yourself and your abilities. Fearing change means holding yourself back from much-needed growth that's important to improving your confidence.

Genuine vs Faking

Showing your real self is a sign of confidence. In other words, being genuine and confidence go hand in hand. You don't have to put on a mask and hide your who you truly are and adapt to what others expect you to be.

Aim to love yourself and be comfortable with who you are – just don't be afraid to show it.

Trying to pretend to be someone you are not produces insecurity, and this is something that can easily be noticed by others. You may find it difficult to create healthy relationships with others since there's a level of trust that might be hard for you to reach if you keep guarding yourself against who you truly are. Everyone knows the feeling of being around someone who is pretending to be someone they are not.

Be brave and always try to be you. But do it not because you're afraid that people might judge you or not accept you, but because you love yourself and you want to be comfortable in your own skin.

Taking Risks vs. Staying in Comfort Zone

Taking risks can be really scary for many, and it's even scarier if you are someone who's not confident about his abilities. Confidence needs to be developed. It is developed every time you choose to accept your mistakes and choose to do things that are beyond your comfort zone.

Recognize your comfort zone and explore these areas a little bit more as it will allow you to also explore the insecurity that lies within you – the insecurity that is possibly holding you back from attaining your dreams.

Building People Up vs. Tearing Them Down

Dragging people down is something insecure people like doing. And this is something that becomes a bigger problem overtime – snowballing from insecurity into a total toxic behavior.

Insecurity is fueled and sustained by negativity. It's necessary in order to endure the voice at the back of your head that's telling you that you're not good enough. Without facing negativity, you'd have to face taking responsibility for your emotions and actions. You'd have to build your confidence.

By trying to motivate others and helping them acknowledge their positive qualities, you're practicing confidence within you. You're strong enough and not afraid to stand next to someone who's successful, confident, and talented.

Sees the Positive in Differences vs. Judgmental of Differences

It's so common for someone who has so much insecurity to judge other people starkly. If you're feeling insecure about a specific part of your life, then you might find yourself judging other people in this area. On the other hand, when you're confident, it's so easy to find good things in others and even hope the best for them all the time. The success of other people motivates you and it brings out the best in you.

This is commonly seen in racism, sexism, and other forms of discrimination. When someone is feeling insecure about himself because of how others are, they tend to be addicted to finding where they fit in.

Making Decision vs. Following

Most of the time, confident people tend to be good leaders. Leading their lives and even others is something that they can do well. Being a leader is something that is inherent, but it is also something that can be earned and developed. If you are a confident leader, people who follow you also become confident.

This is not to say that followers are usually the insecure ones. However, insecure individuals tend to be the ones who usually rely on other people when making decisions. If you find yourself constantly waiting for other people to make decisions for you, then perhaps you need to check on yourself as you might need to start building up your confidence.

Gives Validation vs. Seeks Validation

It's so easy for confident people to give praise and compliments to others. This is because they don't feel threatened by the goodness other people achieve.

On the other hand, when someone comes from a place of insecurity, he tends to always seek validation. A person with so much insecurity tends to feel empty and sad that he thinks that he can't fill in a void in his life if someone else does it first. This can affect relationships because the moment other people are not able to fill that void, this is something that may backfire, which makes the person may feel even more insecure.

Self-Reflection vs. Self-Rejection

Having the ability to just sit and reflect on themselves is probably something that most confident people have in common. These people have no problem asking themselves difficult questions, openly looking at the answers and then using self-development to get better in certain areas in their lives. Being alone with themselves is something that they can do without any problem.

On the other hand, insecurity can manifest in many forms of self-rejecting means. When someone acts from a place of insecurity, he is able to find different creative ways just to avoid the truth about themselves.

Looks for Help vs. Try to do Everything Alone

Confident individuals have no problem asking for help from other people. They are always open to learning new things from others and use their newly-learned skills to their advantage. They are very confident that other people's abilities and knowledge don't negate theirs.

On the other hand, those people who are insecure might act too protective of their own abilities. They tend to feel offended when someone offers help. This makes them stuck in their own ways and hinder their learning.

CHAPTER 3

BODY LANGUAGE

So, do actions really speak louder than words? Can you really rely on someone's actions better than the words they say?

Experts say that most of what we communicate is through our body language, with about 60% to 90% of the way we communicate being non-verbal. These subtle social cues do a lot by letting us truly understand other people's real thoughts and intentions.

So, how can we spot these imperative subtle social cues that explain what's really going on in people's minds?

3.1 The Different Signs to Be Aware of and What They Mean

Whether you are at home, work, or in public surrounded by family, coworkers, or strangers, people's body language speaks loudly. It has been believed that body language establishes over 60% of what people communicate, so being able to learn how to read the nonverbal cues people send is a treasured skill. From how the eyes behave to the direction wherein a person directs his feet, the body language shows what's going on in his mind. In this chapter, I will briefly explain how to analyze body language to better understand the people you interact with on day to day basis.

Study the Eyes

The way eyes behave says a lot. It's important that when you communicate with someone, you must pay attention to whether he makes direct eye contact to you or not. Inability to look someone in the eyes directly can indicate disinterest, boredom, discomfort, or even dishonesty – especially when the person looks away. If someone looks down, on the other hand, it usually means that the person is feeling nervous or submissive. Another thing you may want to notice are the pupils. Pupils dilate every time cognitive effort goes up, so it means that if someone is fixated on someone or something they like, the pupils are automatically going to dilate. The blinking rate of a person can also indicate something about what's going on in his head. The blinking rate goes up whenever people are thinking deeply or are feeling stressed.

Gaze at the Mouth

Pay attention to the movement of the mouth when you're trying to analyze nonverbal behavior. A simple smile can a powerful gesture. As we already know, smiling is an essential nonverbal cue to be aware of. There are different kinds of smiles, which includes real smiles and fake smiles. A real smile means that the person feels happy and enjoys the company of those who are around him. On the other hand, a fake smile usually means they just want to please others by making them think he's happy but they are feeling something else. There's also the "half-smile", which is another common facial expression that only engages a side of the mouth, which can indicate uncertainty or sarcasm.

Notice the Proximity

Proximity is your distance from the other person. Take notice of how close or how far someone is standing or sitting next to you in order to determine if they view you positively. When someone is standing or sitting close to someone, then it might indicate rapport. On the other hand, if you notice someone backing up or moving away when you try to get close to them, then this might indicate discomfort. You are able to tell a lot of things about the kind of relationship two people have by simply observing the distance between them. However, you must remember that some cultures favor less or more distance throughout the interaction, so proximity isn't an accurate indicator of kinship with someone at all times.

Get a Hint from the Head Movement

The speed at which someone nods their head when you're talking may indicate the length or lack of patience. Slow nodding may indicate that the person is interested in what he's hearing and wants to hear more, while fast nodding might mean that the person has heard enough and prefer to stop listening and start talking. Tilting the head on the side while in a conversation might be an indication of interest in what he's hearing while tilting the head backward might be an indication of uncertainty or suspicion. Some people also point using their head or face at people they're interested in or share an attraction with.

Check out the Feet

Our feet are the part of our body where we usually "leak" important nonverbal cues. The reason people involuntarily send nonverbal messages through their feet is due to the fact that they're normally very focused on controlling their facial expressions and upper body resulting in showing important cues through their feet. When they are standing or sitting, a person generally points their feet where they would like to go. So, when you notice that someone's feet are directed in your direction, this could be a great indication that they have a promising opinion of you. This is usually the case for one-on-one interaction as well as group interaction.

See the Hand Signals

Just like the feet, our hands give out imperative nonverbal cues. It's an important area when trying to analyze body language, so make sure to pay attention to this part of the body. When someone is standing, see where the hands are placed. Search for specific hand gestures like where does the person places the hand, in the pocket or maybe on his face. This might specify anything from anxiety to absolute sham. Insentient pointing specified by hand gestures could also speak volumes. When executing hand gestures, a person is going to point in the general direction of the person they're sharing an affinity with.

Observe the Arm Position

You may want to see someone's arms as the doorway to their body. If someone crosses their arms while speaking to you, it's normally seen as a defensive, obstructive gesture. Crossed arms could also specify vulnerability, anxiety, or having a closed mind. If crossed arms come with a genuine smile and overall relaxed position, then it could be a sign of confidence and being laid back. When someone puts their hands on their hips, it's normally used to apply dominance and it is usually used by men more commonly than women.

Keep in mind that the tips mentioned above can provide you with an awareness of the real motives behind someone's behavior, but they are not infallible. When you're trying to analyze one's body language, you have to remember that these methods are not going to be applicable to everyone 100% of the time. There will be aspects like the person's culture and general body language habits that have to be considered in order to precisely decipher nonverbal cues.

3.2 Recognizing People's Intentions

One of the most important skills I've developed in my life is the ability to better understand intentions of other people. Just like anyone who's learning new skills, I have both thrived and failed at this a lot of times in the past. With these trials and errors, I was able to build up myself up to the level where it has become easier for me to judge intentions and motives of people much more clearly, and so their external actions hardly ever affect me emotionally.

Again, let me repeat the fact that the human's body language isn't the same to the way we express ourselves through speaking. A specific movement does not essentially signify a certain word or emotion. There is no such thing as a body language manual or dictionary that is going to help you crack the hidden meaning behind specific gestures. And the truth is, there are no hard and brief rules in terms of understanding a person's unspoken intentions. Even scientists who are trained in the skill of analyzing people make mistakes, particularly when observing someone who's capable of controlling much of their mindful physical behavior.

Gestures are vague. And if you're someone who's good at analyzing others by reading their body language, you know that a certain action can mean different things. If you see someone crossing his arms, it's wrong to accuse him of being defensive because he might be feeling something else – he could be feeling cold or just pretty tired or it could also be an indication that he's feeling comfortable. And it's also possible that the person is feeling all those things at the same time. Yes, it's possible for someone to feel tired, cold, defensive, and comfortable at the same time.

Research shows that no matter what we feel, it first shows up in our body, and then in our conscious minds. So, if we are feeling hungry, angry, happy, impatient, etc., our bodies are aware of it beforehand, and they reliably signal those feelings. Being able to analyze body language, then, is a matter of learning and understanding intents of others, and not their particular conscious thoughts.

So, in this case, how does body language reflect presentation delivery? This works by stressing the points and arguments you are making. In other words, these are the conscious adjustment of your gestures, posture, and expression that are going to underscore and emphasize everything you are trying to say.

Through this, the body language lets you add an emotional length to your presentations. Even though your good posture does not essentially signify a certain meaning, it nevertheless shows the listener something welcoming and positive.

Again, you must keep in mind that body language is not mind reading nor does it provide one an insight into what another person is trying to. All in all, when trying to analyze people's intentions carefully, body language can really be helpful.

Generally speaking, you want to focus on what people want from you when trying to figure out their intentions. However, you're not always going to be able to work out a person's exact intentions, but it is ideal to be able to figure them out in as many circumstances as possible.

3.3 How to Tell If Someone Is Attracted to You

When you're meeting someone for the first time, particularly in a romantic encounter, it's so easy to know as to whether we like them or not – but the question is, how do we know if they like us?

Well, there are some nonverbal cues that easily tell you as to whether or not someone is into you. Here are the body language ciphers you might want to look out for:

❖ **Mutual Eye Contact**

People stare at people they like and if they don't like you, they tend to avoid looking at you directly. The thing that is responsible for increased eye contact is neurochemical oxytocin. High level of oxytocin boosts mutual eye gaze and offers a sense of happiness that boosts mutual attraction. Oxytocin also upsurges pupil dilation that shows interest. The bigger the dilation, the more attracted a person feels toward another person. Throughout the last century B.C., Cleopatra, supposedly the most attractive woman during her time, dilated her pupils with atropine in order to make herself look more sensual.

There's a fine line between bigger staring and eye contact that's impolite. You are able to upsurge mutual gaze by keeping eye contact as you turn your head to disrupt the gaze; the other person doesn't observe your extended gaze as your head is turning. If the person you are with keeps eye contact with you, then there's a big possibility that they like you.

❖ A Gentle Touch

People usually get touchy when it comes to the person they like. In a romantic relationship, the woman might lightly touch the arm of the person they're into. However, keep in mind that this gentle touch isn't an indication that they want a sexual encounter; it merely specifies she is into you. Men express their liking for the same gender by fist bumping or casually hitting the other person at the back shoulder or shoulder. Men equally express their liking for women by doing a playful physical activity. Another type of touching is tidying. Removing lint off of the clothing of another person or fixing their hair or tie might mean they like you. Touching can be a great indicator that a person is into you or not. If you casually touch another person and they snappishly pull away, the person may not like you or just don't want to be too intimate with you.

❖ Inward Leaning

A great indicator that someone you're talking to is into you is body orientation. People lean toward people they like and keep a further distance from those they don't like. Inward leaning reflects rapport. For instance, if there are two people sitting next to one another, their heads will lean toward one another. Next, their shoulders are going to turn toward one another. Furthermore, their torsos will entirely turn as they face each other. Lastly, if two people like each other, then they will lean towed each other.

❖ Mirroring

It's normal for people who like each other to mirror the body positions of each other. Mirroring is able to help develop rapport and could also be used to see whether the person you're talking with is also into you. It delivers a subconscious signal to the person you're with that you are into them; sequentially, they're inclined to like you. When meeting someone, mirror their body position. Eventually, during the encounter, change the position of the body. And if you see that the person also changes his position to mirror you, chances are, they like you.

❖ Barriers

Two people who like each other tend to remove the objects that separate them. Similarly, if two people are not into each other, they feel more comfortable having an object that separates them. These barriers include personal items like newspapers, bags, purses, cups, books, cushions, and any common items around. Having a barrier, however, doesn't necessarily mean that the person does not like you, but it still lets you know that the rapport isn't well established yet. A glass or a cup could be used to monitor liking: If someone you are with puts their glass or cup between you two, it builds a barrier indicating that rapport hasn't yet been established. As the conversation carries, observe where the person puts their glass or cup. If they put it to his side and not in front of the two of you, then they probably like you.

Observing nonverbal behaviors lets you to see the progress of the relationship-building procedure and allows you to know if the person you're with is into you. Nonverbal behaviors also indicate that the person you like, likes interacting with you, which offers a chance for you to develop your relationship under promising conditions.

CHAPTER 4

VERBAL & PARA-VERBAL COMMUNICATION

The difference between Verbal and Para-verbal communication

Of course, you should know by now that communication is a natural phenomenon that naturally takes place between people; it's an act of interaction with people. However, communications don't only come in the form of words. Communication can be both Verbal and Non-verbal.

Verbal communication is the form of communication that uses words to exchange information in the form of speaking or writing. On the other hand, **Nonverbal communication** is the type that doesn't use words. This is done using other forms of interactions. This type of communication may take place with unspoken or unwritten messages like facial expressions, body language, sign language, and others. Now, let's compare the two types of communication to help analyze people better through the way they communicate,

BASIS FOR COMPARISON	VERBAL COMMUNICATION	NON-VERBAL COMMUNICATION
Meaning	The communication wherein the sender makes use of words to convey the message to the receiver is recognized as verbal communication.	The communication which happens between sender and receiver using signs is identified as non-verbal communication.
Types	Formal and Informal	Vocalics, Chronemics, Haptics, Proxemics, Kinesics, Artifacts.
Time Consuming	No	Yes
Probabilities of sending	Rarely happens.	Happens often.

the wrong message		
Documentary Proof	Yes, through voice recording or written form.	No
Advantage	Can easily be understood.	Can easily express feelings and emotions.
Presence	The message can be conveyed through phone calls, letters, etc. so the personal presence of both people does not make any change.	The personal presence of both parties to the communication is necessary.

4.1 Definition of Verbal Communication

The communication wherein the sender makes use of words – may it be spoken or written – to convey the message to the receiver is called Verbal Communication. It's the most effective type of communication which leads to the quick interchange of feedback and information. There are fewer possibilities of misunderstanding as the communication between people is usually clear.

There are two ways to send information. The first way is oral, which can be done face-to-face, phone calls, lectures, and other ways which involve voice. The second way is written, which can be done through letters, emails, text, etc.

Communication can also be categorized into two different types:

- ❖ **Formal Communication:** Also known as official communication, this is a type of communication that uses a pre-defined channel from the sender to convey the details to the receiver.

- ❖ **Informal Communication:** Mostly known as grapevine, this is a type of communication where the sender doesn't have to follow any pre-defined channels to convey the information he has to deliver.

4.2 Definition of Nonverbal Communication

Non-verbal communication is derived from the understanding of both sender and receiver to communicate, as the delivery of messages from the sender to the receiver doesn't involve words. So, if ever that the receiver knows the message entirely and good feedback is provided afterward, then the communication flourishes.

It matches the verbal communication a lot of times, in order to understand the mindset, as well as the status of the people involved but all in all, it's all an act of understanding. The forms of Non-verbal communication are as under:

- ❖ **Chronemics:** Using time in communication is chronemics, which has something to do about the receivers' or the senders' personality.

- ❖ **Vocalics:** The voice's tone, pitch, and volume used by the sender for delivering a message to the receiver are called paralanguage or vocalists.

❖ **Haptics:** It's a communication which involves touching. This is usually used in expressing feelings and emotions.

❖ **Kinesics:** It's the study of a person's body language. It includes postures, gestures, facial expressions, etc.

❖ **Proxemics:** This is the distance kept by a person while communicating with other people; it communicates regarding the person's relationship with others such as personal, intimate, social, and public.

❖ **Artifacts:** The look of a person that has to do about his personality. For example, the way he dresses, carries himself, lifestyle, etc.

Key Differences Between Verbal and Nonverbal Communication

Here are more detailed points that explain the difference between verbal and non-verbal communication:

1. Communication that involves words is known as Verbal communication, while the

communication that is based on signs, is Non-verbal communication.

2. There will be less possibility of misunderstanding when verbal communication is used. On the other hand, the possibilities of confusion and misunderstanding in non-verbal communication are a lot more.

3. When it comes to verbal communication, the exchange of messages is extremely fast that leads to quick feedback. Meanwhile, the non-verbal communication is derived more from understanding that takes time and that's why it's fairly slow.

4. When it comes to verbal communication, it's not necessarily required for both parties to be present because this communication can be done even if both sides are far from each other. On the other hand, people who are involved in non-verbal communication have to be with each other.

5. In verbal communication, the documentary proof can be saved if the communication is done in a formal or written way. However, in nonverbal communication, there's no conclusive proof when it's done.

Keep in mind that Verbal and Non-verbal communication aren't contradictory to each other; instead, they're complementary. In other words, these two types of communications can even go hand in hand for a more effective human communication.

Obviously, verbal communication is an important part of life because words are still the most effective way of communication. However, just like the saying goes, "actions speak louder than words", especially for those who are not able to speak words as well as others, if not, at all – like for babies or people with speech disabilities.

4.3 How to Identify Para-verbal Communication and Language in People

Every time we hear the word "communication", the first thing that probably comes to our minds is probably spoken or written words. But between two people, communication may come in other forms! After all, being seen from the viewpoint of its evolutionary history, this word doesn't stand alone – there are other forms of communication that are also similarly important! In fact, you might have already experienced a situation where you are able to express something or understand someone by just a gaze. Or you've probably experienced talking to someone and thinking to yourself, "I'm pretty sure he's lying". In this case, then you've already used two channels people make use of when communicating with each other and that's what we are going to talk about in this subchapter.

As you probably know, communication is a big part of anyone's life – heck, even animals have their own ways of communication. When you're mad with someone, sometimes, we might choose not to talk. We could simply turn our back to them and they will know what you may want to happen – so, in some way, you did some sort of communication. Letting your body speak for you means you are non-verbally communicating.

This form of communication includes different physical signals used in expressing opinions. emotions, opinions, aversion, and affections. As a rule of thumb, we use them in replacement of our verbal messages. And you probably haven't thought about it, but it's pretty easy to convey a lot of information all on its own.

Generally, using nonverbal communications is pretty quick and straightforward as they're usually made subconsciously and so, they are more genuine and spontaneous. Because of this, a nonverbal form of communication is seen more as a distinct indication of what we truly feel. This gets truly interesting when verbal and non-verbal communication just don't seem to be saying the same thing. For example, when we ask someone the question, "Are you okay?" They say they are, but their actions and facial expressions don't say that they are. In this situation, nonverbal information is seen as more essential and reliable compared to verbal information. This is where the saying that goes "Actions speak louder than words" comes into the picture.

Here are some important fundamentals of nonverbal communication:

- ❖ Distance
- ❖ Gestures and facial expressions
- ❖ Line of vision
- ❖ Objects
- ❖ Posture

Along with the verbal and non-verbal information, there's another means of communicating I want you to be aware of: the para-verbal. This form of communication has all the signals when it comes to dealing with voice modulation and level.

You're probably already aware of this form of communication, and if not, then you should be. When we're certain of ourselves, feel confident, and calm, our voice tends to sound clear and well-articulated. For example, if we feel nervous or aggressive, we tend to speak fast, loud, and high-pitched. Anger and aggression usually make the voice louder. On the other hand, sadness and insecurity manifests itself by a rather more subdued and a higher tone or also by wallowing. Along with insecurity, the level of voice can also express happiness and excitement – you possibly have shrieked for happiness when something really nice happens. On the other hand, fear could naturally lead to some extremely remarkable squealing. As our emotions or feelings change, so does the way we speak.

At present, para-verbal signals aren't completely unambiguous; the subjects of the experiment most easily identify the emotions anger and fear based on the level of voice. From an evolutionary standpoint, this easily makes sense as it was definitely extremely useful that a person was conscious of a danger the other person had noticed in advance or when a person was furious, and so it might be safer to keep distance or to avoid an impending argument. Along with these emotional details, para-verbal signs also give information when it comes to which group we belong to. For example, which dialect we speak or where our accent came from.

When you feel in doubt, para-verbal signals are definitely superior when it comes to verbal content:

when someone tells you he's not afraid of you but says it in a trembling voice, two octaves higher than normal, there's a high chance that he's not telling the truth. Lie researchers have concluded that para-verbal signals could be an extremely effective indication of conscious attempts to lie or deceive people. The wrong modulation, conflicting intonation, or incorrect emphasis immediately warn experts that someone isn't telling the whole truth.

Even though opinions about the reliability of para-verbal and nonverbal signals as a part of communication vary – there's no doubt that these two areas showcase any number of opportunities for misunderstandings and misinterpretation. However, all experts agree to the fact that we impulsively mark the value of para-verbal and nonverbal signals significantly higher than the one of verbal signals. Derived from a research, nonverbal and para-verbal fundamentals showcase about 60% to 90% in response to the question whether a person was telling the truth or not.

If you find this subject interesting, then you'd find this quick exercise fun and useful:

❖ The next time you get the chance to talk to someone, pay close attention to your conversation to their non- and para-verbal signals. What captures your attention the most? Are there specific individuals within your close circle who tend to show incongruent behavior more than others? What do you think is the reason behind this?

❖ Try out the influence you have on others, for example, every time you hold your head up and stare directly into the eyes or contrasted with often casting your eyes on something else and slightly tilting your head forward, what kind of reactions do other people give you that you can easily notice?

❖ Whenever you feel stressed out or insecure, deliberately pay attention to your hands. They usually show the first sign of betrayal whenever you don't feel up to par by fiddling with something or subconsciously touching other parts of our body. If this is something you want to avoid, then find a subject you are able to "hold on to" giving yourself a chance to calm down.

❖ The next time you're going to a bar or anywhere with many people, look at a few people. Notice how you interpret their posture whenever they're taking some sort of actions or movement. Do you think they feel like they're having fun? Do they look bored, tired, uninterested, or bothered? What made you think about those emotions? It is similarly exciting to see people who are trying to flirt? Just for fun, look around and guess which couples might potentially end up being together or having their second date. This could also be a fun thing to do when you are with a friend or two.

❖ If the opportunity arises, it could be quite fun to watch yourself in a video while doing so, you will surely find a lot of things that are interesting!

There are four zones of "personal distance" around people recognized by communication experts. These zones are usually reserved for different types of people:

- ❖ 50 cm - extremely familiar people might get extremely close to us (50 cm).

- ❖ 50 cm to 1.2 meters - people we know pretty well; this can be considered as the intimate zone.

- ❖ 2.5 meters to 3.5 meters - acquaintances and friends where contact stays impersonal and superficial.

- ❖ 3.5 - other people and strangers

If ever somebody who does not belong there happens to go invade our "intimate zone" or even a few centimeters, for example, in overcrowded places, inside an elevator, bus, or concerts, it might make us feel uncomfortable and we try different ways to add distance from these intruders. You will have a lot of chance to do some experiment with your zone. Which distances do you find to be acceptable and those that bother you? Who do you allow to get closer to you? Is there a gender you are more comfortable with? If you want, you can also try to see what happens if you try to intrude into the "intimate zone" of another person – see how they would react.

CHAPTER 5

UNDERSTANDING EMOTIONS

It's a normal thing for us, humans, to read each other's emotions. After all, how many times have you been asked "Are you mad?" by people? If you answer, "Nothing, this is just how I am," people strangely assume that you're actually mad.

But these questions are commonly asked because people actually care about others, especially the ones that are important to them. What do these emotions mean and how are they going to affect us? Do they like us or not? Do we have to do something or just let it be?

The question that usually follows on this extremely practical worry about the feelings of other people is more logical. Perhaps, it comes first at that moment when someone responds to an event amazes you since it is different from the one you currently have.

You're wondering… "Are we feeling the same thing right now?" Which leads to a question that is more general, "Do humans experience or feel the same things as other humans?"

Philosophy has found different answers throughout the years, but in general, the conclusion is that, in general, we are disproportionate with one another. That is a mouthful, but it just means that your experience could be differently from others. Perhaps, I cared more about something and others don't, and that's normal.

Pushing forward, consider individual words. For example, if I say, "Paris" to you, you almost certainly get a mental image of this beautiful city, but what's it based on? Have you ever been to Paris before? I have, so I am definitely more familiar with the city. However, for someone who lives there, the picture of the city in his head will be inevitably more rich, detailed, and a lot more meaningful. The word alone might remind them of their favorite restaurant, their usual bus stop, the office they work at, the park they walk their dogs in, and so on.

Can you say the word "Paris" and mean the same thing to everyone? Not really.

And yet, neuroscience teaches us that people are more alike than are different. For example, recent work on brain scans is able to read human emotions with 90% accuracy. Studies showed people pictures of hostile things – hate groups, physical injuries, and acts of aggression – and it showed how people reacted predictably. But beyond that, their reactions are pretty much the same in terms of brain patterns.

In the same way, a team of psychologists at Princeton University discovered that when a storyteller and a listener come together, the patterns of their brain match up identically. This is to say that stories take over our brains similarly.

Based on brain patterns, human emotions are the same. As the lead researcher, Dr. Luke Chang puts it, human emotions have a "neural signature" that is basically the same among humans. This also shows that computers can possibly learn to identify these emotions with an accuracy of 90%.

And there is one further inference, which is that computer accuracy rate is much higher compared to what humans can manage. And here's more – it is higher even than humans are able to manage *their very own emotions*. We are not even very good when it comes to recognizing our own emotions.

Analyzing other peoples' emotions and also our own is important for great communication. That the study suggests that we're more similar than different shows that humans can lucratively learn to be more accurate when it comes to recognizing emotions and that the results may reimburse in better communications for anyone who tries it.

How to analyse the feelings of others?

Some conversations can get emotional. Even though you have good intentions, you might possibly hurt someone else's feelings without you knowing it. Listening to other people's feelings is one of the best ways to be sensitive with what they feel and to speak to them nicely. It's essential to learn different ways to deal with your own feelings too.

Recognizing Social Cues About Emotions

1. **Observe the person's face.** As you might expect, the face is the most expressive part of the body. If you are trying to know whether a person is happy, sad, lonely, upset, bored, angry, or in pain, you can start by looking at their face carefully.

   ❖ Unlike other social cues, there are seven basic facial expressions that are believed to be universal in expression throughout all cultures. These expressions are surprise, joy, contempt, disgust, anger, fear, and sadness.

   ❖ Facial expressions change quickly and might communicate multiple emotions at the same time. For instance, a person's face might show both fear and amusement if something extremely surprising has ensued.

2. **Be aware of the signs of sadness.** When a person is sad, the face will show it easily. It would not look like a cartoon-drawn picture with his smile showing upside-down, but it will show the corners of his lips to be somewhat drawn down and the jaw comes up.

❖ The inner sides of the person's eyebrows are going be pulled slightly inner and up to the forehead.

❖ Search for the skin below the eyebrows to look somewhat triangulated, with the inner corner going up.

3. **Be familiar with signs of fear.** Being aware of when someone is afraid can help you change your very own behavior. When a person is afraid, his mouth will likely be held open with his lips a little stretched as well as drawn back. His brows are normally high and strained together in one straight line.

❖ Check out his forehead, and search for wrinkles in the middle of the brows, not across.

❖ If a person is feeling afraid, his upper eyelid tends to rise, while the lower lid might be tensed. You will see the upper white of their eye, but the lower might not be visible.

4. **Observe the movement of the body and posture.** Indications that someone is tired might include collapsing shoulders and slackly held limbs. If someone is feeling defensive, you might notice how he may shake his head or cross his hands. If you are aware of these cues, you will be more mindful of the feelings of another person.

❖ If you are not sure if you are analyzing the body language of another person correctly, it is normally fine to ask the person vocally.

❖ But then again, if someone himself is not aware of what he is communicating, you might hear from him that everything is fine when it really is not.

5. **Consider the vocal tone.** Some people naturally moderate the tone of their voice to match the size of the room in order to be heard. If you happen to be in a big room, and the person is talking loudly, it is likely that he is simply trying to be heard. But the use of the same vocal tone in such little space can be a sign of anger, frustration, or even fear.

❖ If someone is having a difficult time to talk, there is a high chance that he's feeling upset or sad.

❖ If he is speaking in an excessively coherent way, then it's possible that he is being sarcastic. Because sarcasm is a means of teasing, it might specify that he's angry but trying to not to make it obvious.

5.1 How to Tell If Someone Has Had A Bad Past and Experiences

All of us have a past, but if someone is going through a childhood trauma well into adulthood, this could be a sign of a bigger issue, particularly in terms of relationships. The influence of childhood on future relationships can be pretty strong, so unless there is some kind of resolution, they may encounter some horrible consequences that may also hold them back from building a healthy, strong relationship.

In my line of work, I constantly encounter people with feeling their absolute best selves, where they can feel comfortable and content in both present and future relationships. An initial step towards having this outlook is to overcome any hindrances you may face in the way, and those can usually be found from the memories of your past or your childhood. If you notice that someone gets too sensitive on a certain subject due to what happened during their childhood, you can try to talk to them about it or encourage them to seek help from a therapist. Through this, they may find a solution that will bring them a feeling of inner peace to move along with their life. The moment they decide to let go, it will be easier for them to put all their energy in their present and future self, and be open and accepting of what life has to offer. Below are the 9 signs a person's childhood has affected his present and future relationships.

1. Insecure Attachment Style to Parents

Mandy Kopplers, a CBT therapist, said that if someone was raised with an insecure style of attachment, they will be more fearful and agitated of having relationships. Adults who carry insecure attachments are likely to be emotionally unstable in relationships. There are some who even have personality disorders with extremely firm, black and white attitude when it comes to relationships with other people. There usually are no grey areas and this has normally developed to pay off for fear of abandonment or rejection. People with an insecure attachment are usually super vigilant to any possible types of abandonment and rejections.

2. Making Present-Day Decisions Based on the Past

After having to deal with a devastating illness, I learned a lot about myself. My main discovery has been the fact that throughout the years, I've been making decisions derived from the labels that were provided to me, or that I believed when I was younger. And this is something I also saw on people who had a problem in their childhood.

3. Trust Issues

It is said that if you find it hard to trust new relationships, this might mean that you are holding onto problems you had experienced in the past. For people who had a dark past, they usually find it scary to open up to other people, always scared that their partner will cheat on them because they experienced it in the past and refuse to believe others when they say that things are all indications of trust issues. They constantly find the need to check their partner's phone or social media accounts and when they find that their partner is paying attention to others, it affects them significantly. The concept of trust is a little hard for them to swallow.

4. Being Mean to Others

Do you notice that every time someone feels upset or anxious, it becomes automatic for them to put other people down? This could be their defense mechanism to make other people feel as bad as them.

5. Too Defensive to People

When they say something offensive to others or do something that makes someone feel bad, they choose not to apologize, rather, they say something that will justify their actions, no matter how much more offensive it might be for others. They find it hard to acknowledge other people's feelings because they might have not experienced being acknowledged for how they felt in the past.

6. Always Leaving First

Constantly leaving relationships could also be a sign of being stuck in a dark past or having a childhood trauma. If you find that someone is constantly looking for reasons to leave and are normally the one to break up a relationship, it may be a sign of having a dark past. The reason for this could be partner or parent's abandonment. So, in order for them to avoid the pain, they find the need to subconsciously abandon or leave first before anyone can do so. They hate the painful feeling of being abandoned but they have no problem making others feel that pain.

7. Being Too Demanding

This negative trait could originate from not being seen and honored as a child. Kids that were put aside or treated unimportantly by their parents as a kid tend to hold onto this fact as they grow into adults. And this unmet desire leads to deep wounding, which puts huge pressure on not just a future partner, but also in future kids.

8. Having A Hard Time to Show Real Self

If you know someone who feels uneasy to express their own thoughts and showing who they truly are, it might possibly mean that they never get the kind of acceptance they need growing up, and up to adulthood, they find themselves searching for approval. A big sign of this is having a hard time to express their real feelings or even be themselves since they were never familiar with an actual parent-child relationship that involves the exchange of feelings, or they were constantly shut down by a strict parent.

9. Parent Went Through a Mental Illness

While this is not the case all the time, if the parents happen to have gone through a mental illness, like bipolar disorder, for example, while they were growing up, they might have been exposed to unstable feelings or a rough, pebbly environment, and people in the past.

5.2 The Best Approach for Handling the Different Emotions

Not long ago, someone I am very close with told me I'm emotionally unstable. Well, I can't say he's wrong. I admit that my emotions can be too hard to handle sometimes, in fact, even for me. I have always been an emotionally-charged individual, and I don't think it's going to go away anytime soon.

While being emotional is something I have no problem with, there are times when other people, who are not as emotional as I, would find it difficult to deal with me. I'm aware that it is probably difficult to know the right thing to say when I am having bursts of emotions, but then again, there are several things that people say that are just not helpful.

Here are some dos and don'ts to remember when having to deal with emotional people:

DON'T: Tell them they are being too emotional.

Well, I'm going to bet that they probably know that. After all, being emotional doesn't come overnight. Most of the time, it has been a part of their personality since they were infants. Calling them emotional wouldn't do anything well. In fact, it might make them even more emotional.

DO: Ask them what they feel.

Of course, they are being emotional, but there are surely reasons why. And you want to try to figure out how they exactly feel. If ever they decide to reveal it to you, it will help them reflect, which, sequentially, might help them feel a little better, at least.

DON'T: Say you understand what they feel when you don't

The truth is, you would not always understand every emotion people experience, and it's okay. It doesn't mean there is something wrong with you. Each person feels differently. By saying that you know how they feel even though you clearly don't, they might feel like you are simply trying to dismiss their feelings as soon as possible because you don't want to deal with them.

No one would like to feel like their emotions or problems are not important.

DO: Say that you want to know and understand how they feel

They might probably tell you that you don't get it, and that's pretty acceptable. At least you told them that you are interested and open to hearing what they feel. There's a good chance that it will make them feel better.

DON'T: Get mad

For someone who's not very emotional, hearing someone cry easily can be pretty frustrating. Being frustrated is alright, but as much as possible, you may want to try not to be obviously upset. By doing so, you'll just make them feel more emotional, but it could also just make everything worse.

Emotional people are emotional – it's not something they can easily control and manipulate. Don't get mad at them; they're probably mad enough with themselves.

DO: Say it's okay

This simple word might come up as cliché. However, emotional people tend to think that there's something wrong with them and it's not okay. Excessive emotions are usually seen as negative, and so, they tend to get mad with themselves when they cannot adapt to this false standard.

Tell them it is okay, and there's no point of getting mad at themselves. They may say that you don't understand them at first, but hearing someone tell you "it's okay" and it's going to be okay does a big thing in making you feel better. Sometimes, validation just does something really big.

DON'T: Try to fight emotion using logic

Logically, yes, they're probably acting silly. Sure, perhaps you have a seamlessly logical solution to their problem that is causing them to be too emotional. However, by trying to fix everything using your incredible logical solution, you're probably just going to make things even worse.

Their emotional state is probably not ready for logical reasoning. Emotions aren't normally logical. On top of this, they are probably not looking for a solution. Instead, they might probably need someone who will listen to them.

DO: Acknowledge that you might not be the best person to help them

Even though you know you can, it's probably better to say that you can't help them. Tell them you might not be able to be helpful in fixing their problem right away, but you are always ready to listen and what they feel is important. Honestly, someone to listen is probably just what they need.

DON'T: Say that it's no big deal

Of course, this is a big deal! Maybe for you, it is not, but for others, what they are experiencing might be affecting all aspects of their life. It's definitely a big deal, although later on, it might be less of a big deal when they start to calm down. When they are at peak of their emotion, it could mean everything to them.

DO: Check in with them later to know how they feel

The fact that you let know that you care about them enough to ask about their emotional challenges and troubles, regardless of how silly they might sound, will mean a lot to them. You, checking back to them will make them feel important, which may even help them when dealing with certain emotions in the future.

DON'T: Talk them down

Don't think that when someone is being too emotional, they are acting like a child. This could be one of the worst things you can tell to someone who is feeling too much emotion. Talking down to people will just make them feel even more upset. So, try not to be a jerk and treat them the way you want to be treated – with respect.

DO: Show a little emotion

Show them that it's normal to feel emotion. Even though you have the emotional capacity of a zombie, just try as much as you can.

Don't be afraid to show that you can also be a bit emotional sometimes. You don't have to pretend to be as emotional as them. A little bit of emotion can do wonder in making them feel they are not alone with the challenges they are currently facing.

CHAPTER 6

PERSONALITY TYPES

So, the magic question that many of us want an answer to is… What really makes a person who they are?

Every person has a unique trait that you can't easily find in others. Experts are trying to figure out the science behind people's personality with individual differences in the way they think, feel, and act.

There are a lot of ways to measure one's personality, but experts have generally given up on dividing humanity precisely into different types. Instead, they concentrate on a person's personality traits.

Five of the most widely accepted of these traits are:

- ❖ Openness
- ❖ Conscientiousness
- ❖ Agreeableness
- ❖ Extraversion

❖ Neuroticism

Conveniently, you are able to remember these traits using the abbreviation of OCEAN, or if you want, CANOE works too.

A team of experts developed the list of traits in the 1970s. This team of two was led by Robert R. McCrae and Paul Costa of the National Institutes of Health and Lewis Goldberg and Warren Norman of the University of Michigan at Ann Arbor.

These traits are the elements that make up the personality of every individual. A person may have a dash of honesty, a great amount of conscientiousness, a standard level of extraversion, adequate openness, and nearly no neuroticism at all. Or you could just be conscientious, neurotic, disagreeable, introverted, and barely open to anything at all. Here is what each trait in this Big Five entails:

Openness

Openness refers to being open to the experience. Individuals who have a high level of openness enjoy what life has to offer. They are inquisitive, imaginative, and know how to appreciate art and new things.

On the other hand, those individuals who have a low level of openness are simply the opposite: They would rather cling to their old habits, try to dodge new experiences, and possibly are not the most adventurous person. It's not easy, if not impossible, for many to change their personality, and this also doesn't happen overnight. However, openness is a personality trait that has been shown to be subject to change as the person gets old.

Conscientiousness

Those who are conscientious are the ones you would normally label as organized and carry a strong sense of responsibility. These people are usually dependable, well-organized, and always have their eyes on the prize. You would not be able to find conscientious people going on adventures on over the world journeys with just their backpack; they are into planning and figuring out what to expect before their trip.

Those who are low in conscientiousness could be expected to be more freewheeling and impulsive. They might tend toward being careless. Conscientiousness is a great trait for a person to have, as it has been connected to accomplishment in school and job.

Extraversion

Extraversion against introversion might be the most identifiable personality trait in the list. The higher the extraversion of a person is, the more outgoing they are. Signs of being extrovert are being sociable, talkative, and being the light of a party. These people tend to be self-confident and cheery throughout social interactions.

On the other hand, there is the introversion that is the opposite of it. These people might require a lot of time alone. Maybe this is because their brains process social interaction in a different way. Introversion is usually confused with being shy and antisocial, but these descriptions are way, way different. Being shy may imply a fear of being in social interactions or an incapacity to function outside their comfort zone. Actually, it's not that introverts can't do well during social interactions; it's just that they mostly prefer not to be in a situation or they like choosing the people they are going to be interacting with.

Agreeableness

Agreeableness measures the level of kindness and warmth of a person. The more agreeable a person is, the more they are likely to be trustworthy, compassionate, and helpful. On the other hand, disagreeable people are usually the ones we label as cold and distrustful of others, and you might have a hard time cooperating with them.

Neuroticism

In order to truly understand neuroticism, you can watch George Costanza of the American sitcom called "Seinfeld." The fictional character, George, is known for his neuroses, which the show explains to be rooted in his dysfunctional parents. He's the kind of person who worries about everything, get anxious a lot over germs and disease, and even quit his job because his anxiety of not having access to a private bathroom is too much for him to handle.

George might be high when it comes to the scale of neuroticism. However, this is a real personality trait. Individuals with neuroticism worry a lot and easily slip into depression and anxiety. It's so easy for these people to find things to worry about.

On the other hand, those who are low in neuroticism level tend to be emotionally stable and think more rationally.

As expected, neuroticism is associated with a lot of bad health conditions. Compared to emotionally stable individuals, neurotic people tend to die younger, possibly for the reason that they turn to drugs, alcohol, and smoking to ease their nerves.

But that's not only it. Perhaps, the creepiest thing about neuroticism is that parasites could be the culprit why some people experience these things. And no, I don't mean the natural anxiety that might come with knowing that a tapeworm has been living in your body. A 2006 study shows that undetected infection by the parasite called *Toxoplasma gondii* might be the reason why some people are prone to neuroticism.

Other personality measures

Even though personality types have gotten out of favor in the modern psychological study as too reductive, they are still well-used by career counselors and in the business world in order to help them form people's understanding of themselves. Maybe the most known is the Myers-Briggs Type Indicator, in fact, you might be even familiar with this.

Myers-Briggs Type Indicator is a questionnaire derived from the work of early psychologist Carl Jung, which sorts people into certain categories derived from four areas: sensation, intuition, feeling, and thinking; and also, two attitudes: extraversion and introversion.

Intuition and sensing refer to how we prefer to collect information about the world, whether it is through sensing or concrete information or intuition or emotional feelings. Feeling and thinking refer to how we choose our decisions. The thinking types tend to run with logic, while the feeling types tend to base decisions on their emotions.

The Myers-Briggs system is made of the judging/perception contradiction, which defines how individuals choose to deal with the world around them. Judging types take decisive action, while perceiving people would rather choose open options. The system identifies 16 personality types derived on the four traits and two attitudes. The 16 different types are the following:

- ❖ The Composer – ISFP Personality
- ❖ The Inspector – ISTJ Personality
- ❖ The Counselor – INFJ Personality
- ❖ The Mastermind – INTJ Personality
- ❖ The Giver – ENFJ Personality
- ❖ The Craftsman – ISTP Personality
- ❖ The Provider – ESFJ Personality
- ❖ The Idealist – INFP Personality

- ❖ The Performer – ESFP Personality

- ❖ The Champion – ENFP Personality

- ❖ The Doer – ESTP Personality

- ❖ The Supervisor – ESTJ Personality

- ❖ The Commander – ENTJ Personality

- ❖ The Thinker – INTP Personality

- ❖ The Nurturer – ISFJ Personality

- ❖ The Visionary – ENTP Personality

Using Myers-Briggs has always been controversial. Research suggests these types don't correlate very *well with abilities or job satisfaction.*

But can personality change?

Possibly. A 2017 study by Psychological Bulletin synthesized 207 published research claimed that one can change his personality with the help of therapy. But then again, this is unlikely to happen overnight, according to a study researcher and a social and personality psychologist at the University of Illinois, Brent Roberts. But he also said that if you really want to concentrate on one part of yourself, and you are willing to go at it analytically, there is now amplified optimism that you are able to affect change in that area.

6.1 Introvert vs Extrovert: Know the Difference

Introversion and Extroversion are two personality traits that are based on specific characteristics. When someone is reserved and doesn't open up easily, chances are, he has an introvert personality. On the other hand, when someone doesn't fear to be a social butterfly, is comfortable in being talkative, and can easily make friends, then there's a huge chance that he is extrovert.

We are the same species with different personalities. It's easy to see the fact that we are the same humans in nature, mind, body, thoughts, emotions, yet we are all unique in our own different ways. It is true what they say, there are really no two people alike, the same way as to how we think, how we feel, and the way we act are different from others, which embodies our overall personality. Now let me give you a breakdown on these two specific attitudes in order for you to know the differences between the two.

Introvert Explained

This is a personality trait where a person is interested in his mental self. Introverted individuals are naturally reserved, as they tend to be preoccupied with their own feelings and thoughts. So, it means that they tend to desire more time within their own private space. In other words, this kind of people feels comfortable and more energized when they're by themselves. So, they choose solitary activities over social interaction and some of the activities they tend to enjoy include writing, reading, listening to music, and making anything related to art. They run a world of fantasies, feelings, and the like.

A lot of people misinterpret introverts and think that they are just being shy and antisocial, but the truth is most introverts enjoy socializing and they are great listeners. They hardly approach people first and they tend to have social anxiety when surrounded by people they don't know.

Extrovert Explained

Extrovert refers to human's attitude wherein a person always like to be surrounded by people. They're confident in a social environment and are very opinionated and straightforward. You can tell that they are the complete opposite of introverts.

Extroverts tend to focus on practical realities instead of feelings and emotions, so being in solitude bores them. So, they choose to be more social, informal, practical, and enthusiastic. Furthermore, their communication skills are outstanding. People who have this kind of personality love social gatherings and being the center of attention is something they enjoy.

As you can see, it's not difficult to distinguish the difference between an introvert and extrovert. While an introvert is not into social gatherings and loves spending time alone, an extrovert, on the other hand, feels pleasure in being socially active, and easily susceptible to being bored when isolated. Furthermore, the introverts are quiet and enjoy listening more while introverts love talking more and being in the limelight.

CHAPTER 7

BEHAVIOUR ANALYSIS

Have you ever given thoughts to how fascinating human nature is? And with the fast-paced life we have, offered by the digital world, understanding the behaviors of other people has become more and more interesting and diverse.

Here, we are giving you some insights on how understanding human behavior helps improve your professional and personal lives alike.

Take a look at human behavior…

For many, it is highly beneficial to gain understanding of their own behavior and thinking in order to gain a better understanding of people around them. Being aware of the reason why someone might be having a hard time with social interactions, or is having difficulty managing emotions such as sadness and fear is something that will be highly beneficial for you when learned fully. The benefits it offers when it comes to promoting positive wellbeing are also numerous.

A level that reinforces you

A lot of careers can benefit from a background that involves reading someone's behavior as this level can help to reinforce the applicant's interpersonal skills like empathy, compassion, as well as motivation. Some of the jobs that might require these skills include the following:

- ❖ Child protection
- ❖ Community health services
- ❖ Human resources
- ❖ Support services

Making a positive change

Individuals who have a strong yearning to help other people and make use of their skills and knowledge to change the lives of others positively to help other people thrive in behavioral studies. Learning how to analyze people's behavior gives us a wealth of information when it comes to human behavior while touching on other parts of the psychology discipline.

7.1 How to Identify and Interpret the Different Types

The way people behave differently makes them unique. And the way we act says so much about who we are. In psychology, our noticeable acts are known as behavior. However, what many people don't know is that behavior comes with different types. Psychology classifies behavior as Overt behavior, Covert behavior, Conscious behavior, Unconscious behavior, Rational behavior, Irrational behavior, Voluntary behavior, and Involuntary behavior, and that's what we are going to talk about in this subchapter.

1. Overt Behavior

This type of behavior is a person's noticeable act. It's pretty obvious that you are able to see it and even measure it at some point. Examples of this type of behavior includes jogging, eating, writing, singing, dancing, exercising, reading, studying, cleaning, etc. You got it. Regardless of what overt behavior it is, it's something that you can observe.

2. Covert Behavior

If overt behavior is something you can observe, covert behavior is a complete opposite. Instead of actions, covert behavior has something to do with one's thoughts. A person may showcase desirable acts like saying he's fine when he's not. Another example of covert behavior is insecurity.

Someone might wear a mask using this attitude. A person with this behavior can easily show different faces in different situations when they want to. This is why finding someone's true personality can sometimes be so challenging. One good example of this is a relationship; many relationships don't last because the partner finds out some untruthfulness about their partner's personality. And most of the time, this is something that can only be learned after years of being together.

3. Conscious Behavior

Conscious behavior refers to someone's intended acts. It's something that you intentionally do. A great example of this is eating a meal or taking a shower. You do these behaviors because you have to. Taking a shower, for example, is necessary before going to work. And eating a meal is of course, important to give yourself some nourishment. These behaviors are consistent with a specific purpose.

4. Unconscious Behavior

Unconscious behaviors are actions that run inevitably without controlling them with your mind. For example, breathing is something we do even when we still and our mind is resting. You might not know what kind of response you will give during a frightening situation. You don't like spiders. They freak you out when you feel them crawling on your skin. Screaming or jumping would be your unconscious response. This is something you didn't even think about.

5. Rational behavior

This category is a type of behavior in psychology that we are able to see among people on a daily basis. It refers to making the decision and actions based on existing social practices and norms. We follow rules because we need to follow them as a responsible citizen. Or we try not to do crimes because it's just something that we should not do. These behaviors are derived from the rationality that we developed to fit in the society we live in.

6. Irrational Behavior

Irrational behaviors are the actions that diverge from what is right. Normally, these behaviors are ridiculous. They don't really serve any purpose. For example, kicking a cat that's walking in front of you in absence of any particular reason.

7. Voluntary Behavior

Voluntary behaviors occur out of the free will. It's the outcome of having the authority to make decisions. You are able to take the course you want in college or just not go to school at all. You are able to focus on working and not let procrastination get the best of you. You can apply for the job you want or leave the job you hate.

8. Involuntary behavior

These behaviors are normally something out of control such as sneezing or the blinking of your eyes when light hurt them. These are the things that you do because you didn't have the chance to stop those behaviors.

In psychology, these types of behavior occur to us on a daily basis. You are able to feel these or observe them in other people. Being open to these types of behavior can be really helpful in analyzing people.

7.2 How to Identify the Different Types of Behaviour and Handle Them

When meeting a sarcastic person for the first time who always criticizes people around him, we will get an impression that he is a plain mean human being. But chances are, there might be a deeper reason for this behavior. What if he acts like that because he feels inferior and he feels like the only way for him to feel superior is to criticize others and make them feel smaller.

When trying to understand the behaviors of others, judging a person based on certain situations rather than linking his behavior to the underlying reasons could be one of the biggest mistakes you can commit.

Understanding people's behavior

Did you have that person in your school who cried after a test because he "only" got 9 correct answers out of 10 questions? You probably thought that he was silly or weird for getting upset with that. But what if he was taught as a kid that being imperfect makes him not good enough and that's a thought he carried until he grew up?

In order to fully understand someone's behavior, you should know that all types of behavior serve an extremely important role to maintain the psychological balance of the person even though the behavior might seem weird.

When parents neglect a child, that child can possibly develop a strange behavior like bullying and stealing. People freak out finding out a kid steals or bully, but do we actually consider why they developed these odd behaviors?

An essential part in understanding the behavior of others is understanding that if the person stopped from doing a certain behavior that helps him keep his psychological balance, then he is likely to develop an entirely different behavior that provides him with the same goal.

For example, if you stop a kid from stealing or if you tell him that stealing is bad, then he can possibly develop a specific type of physical illness with the goal of seizing the lost attention back. For a lot of children who have speech impediment, their stammering can be no more than just a cry for help with the intention of grabbing attention.

Using these examples, we are able to conclude that trying to fix the behaviors of others is all about looking for the reasons that drive them to execute such behavior.

How to Properly Understand People's Behavior

So, is there any specific formula we are able to follow in order to understand other people's behavior?

Well, there are, and they are listed below:

1. Try not to judge someone's behavior without considering their reasons behind those behaviors.
2. The way someone behaves during different situations is going to give an idea of his real intention. For example, someone is talkative because he is planning to run in politics, so he wants to capture people's attention. Or someone shops for expensive things because he wants to be popular.
3. It's impossible to understand someone's behavior before understanding their psychological initiatives. These initiatives are usually formed during their early childhood and are generally kept secret but the good thing is that by connecting the dots, it's not going to be too difficult to learn these initiatives.

CHAPTER 8

PSYCHOLOGY 101

Learning the ability to analyze or read people truly goes a long way. This is especially true if you want to understand or learn the real idea of what someone you're interacting with might have to do with both of your personal or professional life.

People in different professions get training on how they can analyze someone. The obvious roles that need these skills include those in psychology or the ones that are related to health and social services. But there are a lot of other jobs that use different means on how to analyze people. This arrays from salespeople to policemen. Having the ability to analyze others involves paying attention to the smallest details. You have to be able to understand both verbal and non-verbal messages and signs in others.

We all send out a lot of information through the way we move, speak, and act during certain situations. The words we say don't always reflect what we really feel. If you're thinking that being able to read people is only about being able to read what's in someone's mind and see their auras, well, think again! It's not really all about mind reading and knowing what's going on in people's mind. In fact, it's more about being deeply observant. It's about being aware of what body language you need to pay attention to and when.

8.1 FBI's Ways of Analyzing People

It may not come as a surprise for you to that criminal investigators like FBI agents use a combination of psychological, observational, and analytical methods to analyze people. More commonly known as profiling, this process examines through suspects and criminals. If you are a fan of crime TV shows, then you've likely seen this procedure dramatized. But how accurate are they in real life? Well, you can read these real techniques FBI uses and do the comparison yourself.

❖ **Baselines:** There are habits and mannerism that people use on a regular basis. They might be the norm for them, but they might indicate other things to other people. This includes habits such as constant tapping of arms, the crossing of arms, and clearing of the throat. If it is only a specific behavior that can be considered as a quirk, it generates part of their baseline. Other aspects or extreme repetition of actions might show that they're uncomfortable, nervous, or anxious.

❖ **Differences**: The moment you become aware of a person's baseline or normal behavior, spotting the difference would be easier. These usually show up throughout interaction with others. You can start comparing how they're interacting with you, with others, and how do they behave with several people in the room. They also see how consistent their behavior is and how or if they change over time.

❖ **Voices and Language**: The way people talk definitely say a lot of things about them. FBI pays attention to the tone and volume of a person's voice. They notice every word they say, style of language, and jargon they use. Being about to hear analyze the strength or conviction of a person's words can usually say more about the person's thoughts compared to the volume of their voice.

- ❖ **Movement**: See how people move when they're walking. Do they shuffle their arms? How do they position their feet? Where do they place their hands? Do they walk fast? How about the way they stand? Do they slouch or do they look confident?

- ❖ **Clusters**: One type of movement, action, or speaking on its own may not say something out of ordinary. But repeating one movement over and over again or seeing different non-verbal cues taking place all at the same time might. A body that shows this cluster may interpret someone who's feeling anxious or nervous. They might be sweating, fidgeting, and muttering all at once.

- ❖ **Reflections**: There are times when we unconsciously mirror or mimic back the facial expressions or emotions we see in other people. Imitating happens when we're feeling comfortable being around with someone, but also when we are not. When we see someone smiling, smiling seems like an automatic thing to do. When someone laughs, we laugh. When someone's looking sad, we tend to show the same emotion. This is something that people can fake, but usually, they mean well.

❖ **Personalities**: Being aware of people's basics personality traits is a must. This is where the two types usually play a part – are they introverted or extroverted? It's also important to be aware of their decision-making process, what makes them motivated. The way people make decisions and deal with stress and risks can say so much about them and how their mind works.

Psychology Tricks to Analyzing People

Anyone trained in the art of analyzing people's behavior learns and makes use of tricks gathered from psychology. The strategies and skills described in the previous section are essential. This includes having the capability to understand different personality types, find a baseline, search clusters, understand body language and movement, mimicking, and observing how people talk.

In order to have an accurate analysis of other people, you must also know at least a little psychology about yourself too! This includes the following:

Being Aware of Your Biases

In order to analyze other people accurately, you must be aware of your own biases. Your biases are able to affect your judgment. All of us have them. The secret is to be able to know how we can reflect on them and also put them aside while you're trying to analyze someone. By doing that, you stay objective and neutral. For instance, it's human nature to feel empathy or attraction to people who have the same experiences or situations as you.

Making the Most of Your Intuition

Our gut feelings or intuition, no matter what you want to call it, is usually pretty accurate. Never underestimate your capability to analyze a person or a certain situation by trusting in your emotions and especially your instinct. First impressions are very powerful. Most of the time, what we think of someone for the first time is accurate. But then again, always open yourself to other possibilities and reconsider your first impression of other people. Refining in on your capability to analyze people instinctively don't essentially involve intense analysis. You have to be calm and open to what your instinct or gut feelings tell you and have the capability to reflect on what you hear and see.

Appearance

You are often able to tell a lot about someone's personality by just looking at his overall appearance. This is especially the case when you take your time to look at the smaller detail of how people dress and carry themselves. For example, the quality of clothes and fabrics used can reveal the person's level of income. A preference of whether they want casual or formal styles might say something about their personality. Jewelry, accessories, and tattoos may tell something about their hobbies, jobs, interests, and lifestyle.

Context and Environment

It's also very important to consider the environment and context you're observing someone's behavior in. If you see someone sitting in a meeting room with both of their arms crossed, it might indicate that the person is feeling defensive or they're just feeling cold. If you are trying to listen to people talking, do you think their answers are relevant to the topic being talked about and straight to the point? Or you think they are being too detailed and adding information that could have been cut off to shorten their answers?

Facial Characteristics

Another thing that tells a lot about someone's personality is their facial impression. But of course, the finer the details, the easier it would be for you. Check out whether someone has developed permanent frown lines on their forehead or the bridge of their nose from frowning too much. Maybe they developed wrinkles on their eyes because they laugh or smile too much? Do you notice them having pursed lips or clenched jaw, or their mouth is just relaxed? Do you notice their eyes were bright and glistening, sad, dull, or guarded? How easy it is for them to make eye contact?

Touching

The way someone touches other people and the way they touch you, if they do, also tells a lot of things about them. When you shake their hands, do their hands feel cold or warm? Firm or shaky? When they hug you, do they touch your back or just place their hands on the side?

8.2 Understanding Dark Psychology

Dark Psychology is a form of study on the human condition as it links to the people's psychological nature to prey on others driven by criminal or deviant initiatives that don't have many purposes as well as general norms of instinctual motivations as well social science theory. Anyone in the world, regardless of where they are from and what walk of life they are in, has this probability to abuse other humans and other living creatures. While a lot of people restrain this tendency, some simply carry out these impulses.

Dark Psychology is meant to recognize those feelings, thoughts, insights, and subjective processing systems that bring about destructive behavior that is adversative to modern understandings of human behavior. Dark Psychology thinks that criminal, different, and abusive actions are purposive and have some balanced, goal-oriented drive most of the time. And sometimes, Dark Psychology parts from the Teleology and Adlerian theory. Dark Psychology assumes that there's an area inside the human psyche that allows some people to commit terrible acts without any purpose. This theory has been labeled as the Dark Singularity.

Dark Psychology postulates that the entire humanity has a tank of malicious intent towards other people ranging from slightly conspicuous and transitory thoughts to pure psychopathic divergent behaviors which lack any unified rationality. This is what is known as the Dark Continuum. Justifying factors which acts as accelerants and approach the Dark

Singularity, and where someone's atrocious actions fall on the Dark Continuum, this is where it is called the Dark Factor. Short-term introductions to these concepts are explained further below. Dark Psychology is an idea this writer has coped with for 15 years. It has just been of late that he has lastly abstracted the philosophy definition and psychology of this feature of the human condition.

But Del Paulhus has jumped on the trend, with a series of studies probing into the Dark Side of human personality. As Paulhus notes in a paper published in *Current Directions in Psychological Science*:

"Our work on the "dark side" stands in stark contrast to the popular work on positive personality traits. In our view, dark personalities are more fascinating than shiny, happy folks."

Paulhus, along with his colleagues, has counted four different types of selfish and socially violent individuals who many of us deal with in our everyday lives: Machiavellians, Narcissists, Nonclinical Psychopaths, and Sadists. He says that psychologists usually confuse these types of people, who all share a propensity to score particularly high when it comes to lack of empathy. All of these kinds of people also tend to be sociable and extroverted, so they usually make a good first impression, before heading their way to make the life of other people a living hell. But then again, there are great differences, and those differences have important insinuations for the form of harm these people can do to the people around them.

He described Narcissists as *"grandiose self-promoters who continually crave attention."* He also says notes that Frank Sinatra was somewhat a narcissist, which was a trait many artists and celebrities, especially today, in the generation of social media carry.

According to Paulhus, *Machiavellians* are the master manipulators. There are the ones who have cheated us out of something valuable. And they are so good at it that we didn't even notice that they did it until it's too late. Unlike narcissists, they have soaring scores on tests of manipulativeness, and their disposition to be involved in white collar crime is just fairly high. The stock trickster Bernard Madoff, who made his way up to the New York Stock Exchange leadership and used his position to cheat his investors out of hundreds of millions, is a true-blue Machiavellian.

As Paulhus says, *Psychopaths* are "arguably the most malevolent," with high score when it comes to measures of impulsivity, callousness, manipulativeness, as well as grandiosity, which make them a dark force across the board. They usually do harm to other people as they tend to seek thrills without caring much who they will hurt along the way. Because they tend to be impulsive, they are less adept when it comes to white-collar crime in comparison to Bernie Madoff variety, and usually inclines them towards ferocity when other people try to get in their way. Whitey Bulger and Charles Manson are some of the people who had grave cases of psychopathy. However, Paulhus notes that there are a lot of individuals whose psychopathy is pretty low that it's not enough for them to be put in jail.

What is really troubling about this first set, however, is the fact that they are socially skilled and are able to make impressive impressions. For instance, compared to an average person, they are really good when it comes to interviews; this could be due to their high self-confidence and low anxiety level.

Everyday Sadists share the trait of callousness along with other types mentioned. However, the difference is that they are not impulsive or manipulative, but instead, they enjoy cruelty so much. As Paulhus says, this type of people might be drawn to jobs like the military or police officers, where they are able to have the chance to harm other people in a legal way. Paulhus isn't saying, parenthetically, that all people in law enforcement are sadistic; he's just saying that a lot of people in that industry carry that kind of personality.

By reading the paper released by Paulhus, I wouldn't be surprised if you get curious about this author – why on earth would anyone spend their time just to research on psychopathy, narcissism, and sadism? Does he carry the same traits? Well, not really!

Paulhus' interests on the dark side of personality rooted from that same scientific element formed in his mind. In the previous article he wrote on the dark side of the personality, he says that he got into this subject due to his concern regarding "*construct creep.*" He got worried about how many researchers who researched narcissism, for instance, did it without concurrently considering psychopathy or Machiavellianism, would begin to inflate the term to include the other related, but different, ideas.

For Paulhus, it is very important to differentiate the different types of dark personalities as there are real consequences people may face for lack of awareness – a person who is Machiavellian can do a different form of damage compared to the one who is psychopathic or narcissistic, for example. For the reason that these people share a propensity to do well in first interactions, Paulhus stressed that it's necessary that employers use great clean measures of those concepts as part of their personal valuation batteries. And based on what some of many people have told me, some people would have enjoyed having those measurements at hand before choosing their long-term partners.

CONCLUSION

What can you take from this book and how can you apply it?

I'd be lying if I told you that reading one book or a couple of articles would help you analyze someone's personality accurately. As you can tell from what's written in this book, it's a little bit more complicated than that. However, the good news is that with the right knowledge and awareness, this is something that is not impossible for anyone to learn.

If you read this book carefully, you'd know by now how to start. With the information written here and the exercises you can follow, you will be able to analyze someone in no time.

You must also always remember the most important but the trickiest part of the process – getting to know and truly understand yourself as a person. Find out what you really like, dislike, and what makes you tick. Once you fully understand yourself, then you have more than half of the battle won. While every person is different, we are also the same in many ways. After all, we are all people. All of us have the same basic needs.

All in all, you have to know that analyzing people is being able to recognize what's normal and what's not in human behavior. It's not really just about your ability to read someone's mind. Keep in mind that analyzing people is an innate process. Skilled analyzers of other people are known to have a great understanding of human personality traits and nature. They can easily distinguish different situations, and they know that context and time can highly impact one's behavior. They know the meaning behind certain different postures and body languages. Good listening and observation skills are crucial to be able to analyze other people! Equally important is the ability to trust your own perception and understand what you see, hear, and perceive about others.

Now, you can make the move and start analyzing the first person next to you. The moment you find yourself being able to analyze the personality of that person, you can take a step further and start doing it on the first stranger you see.

www.ingramcontent.com/pod-product-compliance
Lightning Source LLC
Chambersburg PA
CBHW070932030426
42336CB00014BA/2647